STEP FORWARD AND SHINE!

Compiled by Rebecca Hall Gruyter
#1 International Best-Selling Author and Publisher

COPYRIGHT 2018

ALL RIGHTS RESERVED

NO PART OF THIS PUBLICATION MAY BE REPRODUCED, STORED IN A RETRIEVAL SYSTEM, OR TRANSMITTED IN ANY FORM OR BY ANY MEANS, ELECTRONIC, MECHANICAL, PHOTOCOPY, RECORDING, OR ANY OTHER, WITHOUT THE PRIOR WRITTEN PERMISSION OF THE AUTHORS.

Table of Contents

FOREWORD 1

SECTION ONE: YOU ARE NEEDED AND HAVE GREAT VALUE 6

Small Steps Count --- 8
By Kimberly Tobin

The Value of a Penny --- 12
By Adrian Jefferson Chofor, CPC

Find Your Spark! -- 18
By Gayle E. Bode

Soul Whispers: A Deep Inner Journey Jena Harris ---------------- 24
By Jena Harris

Financially Step Forward and SHINE Everybody has a gift! What's yours? -- 31
By Marlene Elizabeth, M.Ed.

SECTION TWO: ALIGN WITH YOUR PURPOSE 38

Follow Your Heart and SHINE --- 40
By Nancy Monson, MA, MBA, CPCC

It Only Took A Hyperthyroid, Malaria, and Near Death To Wake Me Up 47
By Susan Jacobs

If You Believe…The Magical Marketer ----------------------------- 54
By Julia Stege, MFA

Step Into Your Passion! --- 59
By Laurie Ratto, RN, HTCP, CCA

Change Your Story; Change Your Life LeaAnn Fuller ------------ 65
By LeaAnn Fuller

The Rise Of The Feminine: 'SHE' Power ---------------------------- 70
By Jennevieve Ybarra, MA

SECTION THREE: STEP INTO YOUR POWER AND PURPOSE 75

Your God is Bigger---80
By Sarah Reilly, CNE, CNC

It's All About Your Attitude -- 87
By Sean Sullivan

Connect To Your Heart (Trust Your Higher Self)------------------ 92
By Phyllis Flemings PhD

Unleash Your Possibility---98
By Mary E. Knippel

Clear the Clutter and SHINE! --103
By Holly Porter

SECTION FOUR: SUPPORT FOR YOUR JOURNEY…………..110

A Unique Way To Shine --112
By Dr. Mary Ozegovich

Three Steps - To End The Overwhelm! -------------------------------118
By Mary Shores

The Truth about Hormones ---124
By Dr. Liz Lyster, MD, MPH

Money Talks! Prevent Yours FrBom Saying Good-bye!--------- 132
By Robert & Deanna Goldsmith

The Three Secrets To Business Success Revealed! -----------------141
By Dr. Greg L. Alston

Creating A Legacy Through Wellness Rosie Bank ----------------147
By Rosie Bank

SECTION FIVE: STEP FORWARD!..154

Shining with The Celestial Spoon -------------------------------------156
By Catherine M. Laub

Live in Alignment to Fulfill your Purpose ---------------------------163
By Naomi Bareket, MBA

Choose Freedom Over Fear of Judgment ---------------------------170
By Kimberly Schehrer, MA

Step Powerfully ---176
By Jaimie Harnagel

Is It Me, or Is It You? --183
By Jacque Opie

SECTION SIX: CHOOSE TO SHINE! **188**

Technology With A Heart Michelle Calloway -----------------------190
By Michelle Calloway

Create Your Blissful Life Moneeka Sawyer --------------------------196
By Moneeka Sawyer

The Final Gift Dr. Ruth Anderson ---------------------------------202
By Dr. Ruth Anderson

Lessons I learned from Fifth Street -------------------------------208
By Cassandra F. Garabedian

Leveraging that Magic Moment Step into Your Light ------------ 214
By Jeanne Alford

From Garbage to Gold ---220
By Kari Kelley

A NOTE FROM REBECCA **226**
REVIEWS **228**
CLOSING THOUGHTS **234**

Acknowledgements

When writing an anthology, it takes many voices be willing to join together to bring forth the book in a powerful and united way. It has been such an honor and privilege to work with this amazing group of authors. I want to thank these amazing authors for entrusting us to bring forth and share their powerful chapters.

I want to thank my husband for always cheering me on and encouraging me to SHINE! I thank God for giving me opportunities, opening doors, and bringing together the right people for this powerful project. I thank my parents for their love and support and my grandmothers for planting the legacy seeds to always choose to Bloom, Step Forward and SHINE!

Foreword

"Step Forward and SHINE!"
By: Rebecca Hall Gruyter, Book Compiler

Thank you for leaning into Step Forward and SHINE! I'm honored and excited to bring this powerful book to you, featuring over 30 experts that are committed to helping you SHINE powerfully in your life!

As a women's empowerment leader, I know a lot about being disempowered and how to overcome that in order to step into your passion, power, and gifts so that you SHINE! I celebrate you saying 'yes' to this book and to yourself! It is a courageous act to say 'yes' to you and to be willing to let others walk beside you to support and cheer you on in life.

In sharing their stories, our authors will equip and empower you to discover your value, align to your purpose, step forward, and choose to SHINE! I believe this book is a living and interactive book that will speak wisdom, encouragement, and power into your life. Your heart will be touched and you will be motivated and to take action to step forward powerfully in your life. I want to invite you to pause, take a deep breath, and be ready to receive these powerful stories and messages so they can ignite a fire in you, inspire courage in you, and focus your purpose in your life to encourage you to take action now and SHINE!

I'm passionate about women stepping forward and sharing their wisdom, heart, lives, and stories because I know firsthand what it like to come from a much-disempowered place. I experienced all types of abuse during my most formative years – the tender ages of 5 to 13. I actually continued to visit that abusive environment until the age of eighteen. This environment of abuse made me believe false messages like: "I am not okay," "there is something wrong with me," that it must be "my fault," and that it is "NOT safe to be seen or heard." As a result, I became an expert in hiding. When I was finally rescued by my birth father and placed in his home with my stepmother (who became the mother of my heart), I was able start my healing journey. On this journey, I discovered that these previous beliefs I had embraced in that unsafe environment were actually lies. I discovered that I am beautifully and wonderfully made (just like you), on purpose and for a purpose; that I matter and am needed just as I am; that it wasn't my fault; and ultimately that it is safe to be seen, heard, and SHINE!

So, my mission - the calling of my heart - is to help others understand same truths: **We are all beautifully and wonderfully made and needed just as we are.** When we step forward and share the gift of us, it makes a difference in our lives and in the lives of those around us. This means we have to be willing to be seen on the same level that we are wanting to serve and make a difference in the world. **The more you SHINE, the more you are paving the way for others while sharing the amazing gift of you with the world.**

My heart's desire and calling are to equip and empower you to step into the center of their lives - not just living life as a supporting character or a role we can hold in life. rather, I want you to really step forward fully in your life. Bring it all; authentically and powerfully share your story, life, and heart with others. Some of the greatest gifts I have been given are by women and men who invested their life and heart in me. This book is allowing us the opportunity to pour into you. To support, celebrate, and to encourage you to *Step Forward and SHINE!*

We each need others to encourage us, to speak wisdom and truth into us, to love us and cheer us on, and to help us stand up again when we fall. This book will walk beside you to help you run and not grow weary, to complete all that you are called to complete, and to SHINE in your life and business!

In creating this book, I asked each heart-centered and powerful co-author to share some of their personal story and journey with you. As they share from their respective journeys with you, they share what they have learned. They share their wisdom and what they wish someone had encouraged them with or whispered in their ear - especially in those dark and challenging times. They are committed to pouring into you, to equip and empower you in your life. Throughout the chapters you will feel a consistent and transparent heartbeat to support you in very real ways as the authors often share what they wish they would have known. We want to make your path and journey easier for you step forward and SHINE! As the book compiler, I'm so proud of what each co-author has shared in their chapters, and am honored to have each of them leaning in to support you.

I am equally honored that you have said "yes" to our book and are entrusting us to support you on your journey.

Now it's your turn. Are you going to lean in and learn from the wisdom within this book? Will you let us walk beside you on your journey of life? We want to lift you up, support you, encourage, and empower you. It is your choice. We want to be equipped and empowered to take action, move forward and share your gifts with the world. You can choose to open the pages and let them pour into you, or you can put this book on a shelf. My heart and prayer are that you will say "yes" to you and lean into the powerful messages of hope that are waiting to pour into you, your heart, and your life.

You have unique gifts, talents, abilities, stories, journeys, and perspectives that you alone can bring forward. Those in your life need you, your message, your wisdom, your perspective, gifts, talents, and heart. When we shrink back or hide, the world becomes less vibrant and we all miss out. Be willing to share the gift of you with those around you and with the world! Be willing to be seen on the same level you are willing/wanting to serve.

Here is how to get the most out of this powerful book. It is divided it into six sections, each one designed to meet you exactly where you are at and to support you to Step Forward and SHINE: **"You are Needed and Have Great Value"**; **"Align with Your Purpose"**; **"Step Into Your Power and Purpose!"**; **"Support for Your Journey"**; **"Step Forward"** and **"Choose to SHINE!"** I encourage you to pick the section that pulls at your heart the most each time you pick up the book and then select one or two chapters in that section to support you with the focus that will be of the greatest support you to each time you open this dynamic book. You will find, at the end of each chapter, the contact information and a little bit about each author. I know that they would love to hear from you, to know how their chapter supported you, and to build a connection with you through social media, etc. I encourage you to "friend" and follow those authors with whom you feel a powerful resonance and connection so that they can continue to pour into and support you on your journey in life.

Now the next step is yours. Drink-in these stories and messages that are within these pages to serve, support, and inspire you. Take the time to pause, read, and reflect. Listen to the powerful messages of hope that are waiting for you within the pages of this book. It's not an accident that you purchased this book and are opening it to read right now, today. I invite you to lean in and truly receive the messages and wisdom that will speak to your heart and soul that you will find in these transformational and dynamic pages. Enjoy this rich collection of wisdom, love, encouragement, so that you can Step Forward and SHINE!

-----Rebecca Hall Gruyter, Book Compiler

Founder/Owner of Your Purpose Driven Practice and CEO of RHG Media Productions

Rebecca Hall Gruyter is an Influencer and Empowerment Leader committed to bringing Experts and Influencers forward so that together we can lean in and make the world a better place one heart and life at a time. She is the owner of *Your Purpose Driven Practice*, creator of the *Women's Empowerment Series* events/TV show, the *Speaker Talent Search*™, and *Your Success Formula*™. Rebecca is an in-demand speaker, an expert money coach, and a frequent guest expert on success panels, tele-summits, TV, and radio shows.

As the CEO of *RHG Media Productions*™, Rebecca launched the international TV Network (www.RHGTVNetwork.com) to bring even more positive and transformational programming to the world. In July 2017 she launched the Global RHG Magazine & TV Guide bringing inspirational influences to the world and their messages! In January 2017, she expanded RHG Publishing to now help individual authors bring their books forward as best sellers so they can be positioned as they bring their powerful book forward.

Rebecca is a popular and syndicated radio talk show host, #1 bestselling author (multiple times), and publisher who wants to help YOU impact the world powerfully!

Contact Information:

(925) 787-1572

Rebecca@YourPurposeDrivenPractice.com

www.facebook.com/rhallgruyter (Facebook)

www.YourPurposeDrivenPractice.com (Main Website)

www.RHGTVNetwork.com (TV Network)

www.SpeakerTalentSearch.com (Free Opportunity for Speakers to get on More Stages)

www.EmpoweringWomenTransformingLives.com (Radio Show)

www.MeetWithRebecca.com (Calendar link to schedule a time to talk with Rebecca)

SECTION ONE

YOU ARE NEEDED AND HAVE GREAT VALUE.

In this section discover how valuable and important you are. You, your gifts, talents and abilities are absolutely needed for such a time as this. You are a gift to all of those around you!

Small Steps Count
Kimberly Tobin

Wow! How did it get to be this time of year again so quickly?! Today, Adam (my son) and I are going Christmas shopping for the presents he needs to get for his friends and family. I really am excited to spend time with him! So why am I so freaking stressed out?

Here we are in a big box store in the middle of the weekday within ten days of the holiday. My favorite time of the year and I'm cranky. "Mom, calm down!" My two favorite words, NOT! If someone is upset, the words CALM DOWN are not what you want to hear nor do they help at all. Deep breathe Kim!

Once again, he is right. I love seeing the world through his eyes. Adam is twenty-six and was diagnosed with Asperger's Syndrome over ten years ago. His view of this world reminds me that simplicity is often best. He is high functioning and is a genius with a black and white view of this world, right is right and wrong is wrong. He doesn't see the need to lie, even a little bit. If it's not true, then don't say it.

In Adam's world, "Adulting" officially stinks! He questions the need to go to a JOB every day that you hate just to make money and pay for necessities. In his mind, life should be fun, adventurous and not spent on things you hate! We have had many conversations about working for an employer that you don't like. Adam questions the feeling of the money you earn doing what you don't enjoy and I totally agree. His point of view is if you receive money doing what you don't like then what you pay for with that money will be on things you don't like, creating an environment you don't like. So, what about using this money to buy things you think will make you happy? We agree that this is the long way around being happy.

One thing that is very clear, Christmas is for giving presents friends and family enjoy and not for things they need. So, let's get into the spirit of the season! We both truly love Christmas and I say a quick prayer that I am present and enjoying our time together! "Please, Dear Lord, send us something special to remember this day."

We start piling our basket high with thought-filled gifts for everyone on our combined lists. If I do say so myself, we have been very creative with our choices! Nothing is more fun than to give a gift that you know someone will love and cherish.

Two hours have passed quickly. We are laughing, singing and remembering Christmas gifts of the past. "This is what the Christmas time is all about, Adam." He just grins from ear to ear having as much fun as I am. We head to the checkout line and wouldn't you know it, every checker has a backup of customers. I start to stress knowing this is going to take a while. Why am I stressing, again? I have planned to be with Adam all day. No other appointments to get to other than lunch. It's all good. I remind myself to decompress as my emotions affect him. Not just him, our emotions effect all of those around us.

While we are standing in line, the lady in front of us is checking out. She is elderly and using a cane to assist in walking very slowly. Her grandson is helping her. But what is taking so freaking long? Breathe Kim! As I inch closer, I can see that she is trying yet another credit card to pay for her things. Oh, I've been there before - nervously wondering which credit card will work, begging internally to please let there be one that does work.

I hear her telling the clerk that she is in from out of town to celebrate the holidays with her son that she hasn't seen in many years. She just needed a few things. And she tries another card that is being declined.

I try not to listen. This is an embarrassing moment. I know first-hand! I notice the items she has checked out and I look at my basket. My items are just gifts, not necessities.

I hear a voice inside me saying "pay for her items". "What? NO." I don't want to embarrass her. She probably won't let me. The voice persist, "pay for her items". This is not the first time I have heard this voice. It's soft yet stern and I know deep inside of me that if I don't pay for these items, I will truly regret and beat myself up for EVER!

Have you ever had those moments…where you get that inner prompting, resist but know if you don't honor it you'll regret it? This was one of those moments.

I take a deep breath. "Excuse me, ma'am. How about I pay for your items as a Christmas gift to you and your family?" There, I said it. She's not going to let me, but at least I offered. I look back at Adam and his eyes are so big with appreciation for me. I didn't plan on that.

She turned to me, tears in her eyes and said the most heartfelt "Thank You" I have ever heard.

She said, "You are a God sent Christmas Angel. Can I give you a hug?" I replied with my arms stretched out, "absolutely! I am happy to be able to help!" She proudly turned and introduced her grandson who give me the biggest bear hug! I introduced my son just as proudly. He stretched out his arms and hugged her too. She said, "you have a very special Momma, you know that?" Adam proudly replied, "Oh, I am very aware how great she is!"

I completed her transaction and gave her the receipt as we said goodbye. I checked out our Christmas presents thinking how amazing it was to be able to help someone in that way. My heart was so very full. That I could help a stranger even with my doubt and second guessing. What a powerful moment to be seen that way by my son and make a difference for someone. I didn't have to be perfect, just willing.

We filled out cart with bags and I signed the credit card receipt. It was a receipt that shows a total how much you saved on your items purchased that day. Guess what? The amount I saved was less than ten cents difference from the amount of the elderly lady's total receipt.

As we left the store, my son turns to me and shares: "Mom that was the coolest thing EVER! I'm so proud of you! You truly do make a difference in peoples' lives everywhere you go. Sometimes you do it with just a smile or hold open a door and sometimes you do something so big you make them cry. I just love you!"

"You watch me?" "Yep" he replied. **And you know what else, Mom? That, what you did today, stepping up to help, is what Christmas time is all about!"**

Wow! He watches me. The things I do that I think no one else notices, he does. <u>**He again reminds me that simple is best, small can be big and all you have to do is try.**</u>

It's easy to get lost in feeling that one person can't change the world. You can, in fact, only change one person, yourself.

As a Spiritual Coach, I witness clients in the midst of burnout, full of fear and doubt without a clear direction. **I often learn their frustration comes from expecting to change the world in one day. It's a huge burden** lifted when we map out a path that includes small steps, but still moving forward. **No need to jump off a cliff. Just take a step, even a small one.** Smile at a stranger, hold open the door for someone you haven't met or buy a coffee for the person in the drive-through behind you.

Here are some lessons my son has taught me:
1. Simple is best
2. Small can be big
3. All you have to do is try
4. Remember to breath
5. Just take a step (remember small steps count)

About the Author

Kimberly Tobin is a transformation mentor; business strategist, International Best-Selling Author and speaker helping Spiritual women clearly acknowledge and embrace their unique gifts that fears often conceal. She is passionate about helping women strengthen their connection to Spirit enabling them to celebrate their Divine inner magic and create the life they boldly desire. Kimberly is direct and honest with her clients, enabling great changes to manifest quickly. She reminds us that even though a spiritual path is personal, you do not have to do it alone. Kimberly works with her clients from her office in Missouri offering transformational programs as well as private, one on one intensive session in beautiful locations around the world. Learn more about Kimberly at www.KimberlyTobin.com.

Email Address: Kim@KimberlyTobin.com

Phone Number: 314-267-3081

Website: KimberlyTobin.com

https://www.facebook.com/kim.f.tobin

https://www.linkedin.com/in/kim-tobin-47653618/

https://twitter.com/Clarity_Kim

The Value of a Penny
Adrian Jefferson Chofor, CPC

As a young child, I was considered a 'dreamer' with my head drifting merrily in the clouds miles away from my surroundings. My dreams took me all over the world to meet all of the fascinating people that were pictured in the worn pages of the family's World Book Encyclopedia set that I read religiously. Reading and sleeping were the only escape I had from the combative household I grew up in.

I was close to my father, but he did not care to hear about my glorious adventures of escape to the far-flung corners of the earth. My mother's cold, emotional detachment, and disdain for me became the mainspring for my imaginative departures to exciting places where I was accepted and felt safe. My four older brothers were very popular in the suburban New York City area I grew up because of their charisma, athletic prowess, and good looks. Although I was good in sports and was an affable kid, I was more introverted and stayed nestled in their long cast shadows.

That didn't mean that I didn't stand out. I was always the tallest in my class and by the time I was in kindergarten I was wearing a size-5 ladies' shoe! My stature should have been a source of pride, but to an African American girl living in a predominantly Italian, Irish and Jewish community, I was often made fun of because of my height. It didn't help that I suffered from, cystic acne and hyperhidrosis. These conditions not only made me highly self-conscious but led to awkward social situations triggering anxiety attacks. **Yes, I stood out, but didn't shine! I was like a filthy penny covered in debris and rust lying on the ground waiting to be picked up by an eagle-eyed pedestrian looking for discarded coins or discovered by accident.**

When I became a teenager, I started to attend a high school in the City, and it was there that I entered what was to be labeled as my 'rebellious' stage. I was constantly getting into my fights with classmates and girls from neighboring schools. It wasn't that I enjoyed fighting, but it became an outlet for all of the repressed rage I had for my mother and growing up in a contentious household. The problem got so out of hand that I received a Superintendent's Suspension for breaking the discipline code for serious offenses. My mother who had not taken any interest in me for most of my school age years, except for verbal criticism or corporal punishment, was the one to accompany me to the Superintendent hearing. **She announced to no one with a tone of contempt that I was the worst child that she had ever had.** Each word rang out in the hearing's chamber as clearly as a church bell being rung from a medieval cathedral on a serene Sunday morning calling sleepy parishioners to worship. **This pronouncement only fueled my rage and soon after I ran away from home.**

I was always confident that my father would search for me to bring me home. He would plead with me, school administrators, counselors, and anyone that would listen, to help me before he lost me forever. The man was at my school so often, he was mistaken for staff on more than one occasion and knew the security and administrators by name. I was 16 years old, the last time that I ran away from home. I told my father that when I turned 18, I was leaving for good. I would daydream about living in Paris and living the life of an expatriate. I imagined ordering the most scrumptious, crusty baguettes and dipping them in whipped butter, not the tasteless margarine that I was accustomed to eating. I am a fancied myself living in a grand apartment with a view of the Eiffel tower. **My dreams of living abroad never left me, even during my darkest moments; I knew that one day I wanted to live overseas.**

True to my word, soon after I turned 18 years old I moved out of my parent's house without looking back. I thought my nightmares were over, but I was about face some of my greatest tests. **One of my darkest moments was a brief period of homelessness late spring 1993. I felt utterly alone and ashamed. I remember thinking, "Was I too presumptuous for leaving home so young?"** I could hear my mother's parting words haunt me. She said, "Once you leave, you can never come back!" **My shame enveloped me like a cloak rendering me numb and feeling invisible by those around me. I was becoming used to feeling like the corroded penny lying in debris on the side of the road. <u>I made a promise to myself that I would never be homeless again!</u>**

By God's grace and determination; I got on my feet and by the year 2003. I lived out of a suitcase not because of homelessness, but because I was constantly traveling. If there is one gift my mother gave me is the love of travel. My mother was a travel agent for almost 40 years and experienced traveler that has stepped foot on every continent except for Antarctica. She shared with me an insatiable need for traveling and I am grateful for that gift. Traveling has helped me to get out of my comfort zone, experience new cultures and be a more open-minded person. **As someone that felt like an outsider all my life, travel was never about escapism, but a way of connecting with others like me or looking for a place of belonging. That feeling of connecting and belonging led me to moment that would change my life.**

In March 2003, I was in beautiful Rio de Janeiro, Brazil. The moment I stepped off the plane I felt like I was 'home.' **It didn't feel like I was visiting Rio, it felt like I was returning home.** It was during this first trip to Rio that I experienced a paradigm shift from the notion of traveling to residing abroad because I did not want to leave. I returned to Rio de Janeiro and visited other parts of Brazil and I knew that I had to leave the States because living abroad is where I should be. During this time, I was also visiting Europe. I loved visiting my friends in Italy, Spain, and England and really enjoyed my time there.

In early 2004, I started seriously contemplating moving out of the expensive apartment I was renting and buying a property outside of the United States. **But, my yearning to move abroad would leave me conflicted and confused. I was unsure what I my next move should be. That is when I decided to stop allowing external pressures and expectations dictate what was best for me but stop and listen to my inner wisdom and let its voice tell me.** The voice started with a whisper that grew louder each day until it could no longer be ignored! I knew that the right path for me was to move overseas, but where?

After much prayer and deliberation, I settled on relocating to Rome, Italy. My target date was May 2005. There were many months of planning that included, material downsizing, a TEFL course to become an English teacher, police clearance for visas, opening & closing bank accounts. That is a very short list of the many things I had to do to prepare for my move. **What I had not prepared for was the negative and less-than-encouraging response I received from my friends and family. I presumed they would be happy for me and cheer me on, but the response I received was overwhelming negative.** Many people could not fathom why I would want to leave the United States. Some of my African American friends did not understand why I chose a European country to reside. Others told me that I needed to settle down and think about getting married and starting a family. **I was shocked that some actively tried to dissuade me from living my dream. I knew more than ever that I needed to pay heed to the voice of my inner wisdom.**

The exhilaration I felt when at May 31, 2005 I arrived at Fiumicino airport outside of Rome, Italy. My life as an expatriate in Europe began! **All my life I had dreamed of living abroad and FINALLY I made it a reality! All because I listened to my inner voice**, set goals, and with sheer determination made it a reality. One outstanding lesson I learned is to value myself! I always considered myself to be like the dirty penny that was tossed in the gutter, but later I started to understand and appreciate my value much more.

If you happen to have a genuine penny dated 1943, then I want to share a little bit about its value. The 1943 penny is that it's the only regular-issue United States one-cent coin to be minted from steel to save copper for World War II ammunitions. Officials with the US Mint had to find a way to replace the copper in one-cent coin with low-cost material. They determined zinc-coated steel to be the best choice. Although a creative solution, the public confused the silver-colored pennies with dimes and the steel inside the coin was prone to rust after exposure to moisture. The US Mint reverted back to copper utilizing metal from spent copper shell casing to mint Lincoln pennies. The 1943 copper pennies are believed to have been accidentally made from a few remaining blank copper planchets (round metal disks). The blanks were unintentionally fed into the coin equipment along with steel planchets, resulting in the creation of a couple of dozen rare 1943 copper cents. The value of a 1943 copper penny is now worth more than $80,000 today!

For many years, I undervalued myself and failed to appreciate my worth, choosing to believe that I was not worthy of love and attention. I always stood out but, the sad, lonely girl would not allow herself to shine choosing instead to walk in the shadows of others. **I needed to change the perception of myself and stop thinking of myself as filth covered penny with little value, but as unique and valuable like the 1943 copper penny! Our unique stories are powerful and our life experiences are priceless.** This is one of the reasons; I became an empowerment coach to help women tap into their inner wisdom and true authentic self to explore their full potential. I am passionate about helping them see their real value and accept themselves for who they really are. **After personally experiencing transformational change, I am convinced that empowering women and helping them to step forward and shine is *my* purpose.**

Here are the steps I discovered that will help you step into your transformational change:

1. **Get Clarity**

   One of the first steps I took in my transformation was to get clarity. I needed a clear vision of what I wanted and where I was going. No dream is too BIG!

2. **Set Goals**

   The next step was goal-setting. Imagine you have an elephant that you need to eat. How do you do that? 'One bite at a time, of course' 'You' have a BIG dream, but it will take small steps or SMART goals to achieve reaching that dream. Then you will think of all of the options you have to attain your dream.

3. **Take Action**

   Last, but not least – **DO IT!** Be your biggest cheerleader and listen to your inner wisdom as it drives you to live your purpose!

   The meaning of life is to find your gift. The purpose of life is to give it away – Pablo Picasso.Share your story, your life, and your gift. This is your purpose.

About the Author

Adrian Jefferson Chofor is the CEO and founder of Aspire2Inspire Transformational Practice, LLC, and a life coaching practice that transforms client aspirations into reality with inspirational outcomes. Adrian, a certified professional coach, established Aspire2Inspire Transformational Practice with the mission to empower women to transform their lives and lead their lives with passion and purpose.

As an empowerment and performance coach, also known as 'Your Empowerista,' she is recognized for her ability to motivate under-performing teams, increase productivity, and be a change agent. In 2017, she received an innovation award from Kaiser Permanente, an innovation leader in the healthcare industry. She is now focused on empowering its members and employees to share their powerful stories to inspire others.

Adrian is an entrepreneur, international public speaker, and mentor with over 20 years of professional experience in executive support in healthcare, publishing, and academia. She is a travel enthusiast having visited over 20 countries in Europe, South America, Africa, and the Caribbean and a former expatriate that has resided in Italy, Spain and Germany. Her passion for travel inspired her to start her own travel agency, Aspire to Cruise and Travel LLC in 2015 to help transform client's dreams into one-in-a-lifetime trips and unforgettable experiences.

She is an avid runner, lover of beach and seafood, and all things Kauai and Barcelona. She is a mommy to two adorable children and an intelligent, sensitive, and caring son and a spunky, fearless girl that is a born-leader. Bossy no - A Boss, yes!

connect@adrianjeffersonchofor.com

925-727-2453

www.adrianjeffersonchofor.com

https://www.facebook.com/adrian.jeffersonchofor

https://www.facebook.com/YourEmpowerista/

https://www.linkedin.com/in/adrianjeffersonchofor/

https://twitter.com/yourempowerista

Find Your Spark!
Gayle E. Bode

I greatly appreciate my life today. I have so much for which to be grateful. My family is healthy and happy. My children are doing well for employment, relationships, and have happy homes. I have designed the business of my dreams and get paid to do what I love. Life is good! However, it wasn't always like this. In fact, I'm going to share some of my story with you of when I lived in fear, lost my spark and how I rediscover it.

I know that I am more than what I do for a living. It is as if divine timing is sitting on my shoulder. I can feel the divine guidance and supporting angels. I truly have everything I need. What's more, I know I can get more whenever I need it. I have learned that I do not have to do everything by myself. However, I do need to love and trust myself. **This realization "my spark," has made an enormous difference for me in my life. My wish for you is that you discover your spark as well.**

I thought for a long time that I must work harder and do more. I felt that I always needed to make up for anything I did not do correctly or completely accurately. I was consistently in a place of trying to make up for what I perceived was lacking in me. I worried that I was not doing enough all the time and because of that, everything I worked for would suddenly fall apart. Let me share some of why I felt this way.

I survived a very devastating divorce. I was told by the Judge that I had 30 days to vacate my home. My husband of 18 years claimed he never owned the property where we lived and that his mother was kicking me out. And had calculated an amount I would owe for back rent for every month of every year I had lived there. So, I really did lose everything then. A few years later, I married an award-winning chef in San Francisco. He turned out to be dealing drugs out of the back of the restaurant at 3:00 in the morning. I kicked him out of my life, but not before he left me tens of thousands of dollars in debt. This was followed by three years of death threats, which resulted in having to move my three children and me to another state in order to be safe. **I lived in very real fear and I let my fears control me.**

Thankfully, life is not a solo journey. Many good and trustworthy people helped me along the way. I did not have to do life all by myself. I could get help, and I did.

I learned a lot about myself, how I think, respond, and problem solve. I took lots of classes on getting centered, gaining clarity and healthy expression of what I really want in life. I learned what is of ultimate importance to me. I took personality tests, classes on My Inner Magnificence and studied my Chinese horoscope. I got a reading from the Akashic Records. I got traditional mental health counseling, holistic healing, tapping, and hypnotherapy. In counseling, I learned to write out thought patterns and ask if what I was telling myself was my voice or someone else's. All these different techniques helped me rediscover my true self and inner wisdom…my spark. I reconnected with what is really important to me. I discovered how to understand and accept my unique gifts, talents, and way of thinking.

A turning point came through the class on discovering my values. In the class, we started with a list of words that resonated and best described us. My words were: pioneer, honest and caring. We looked up each word in the dictionary. I spent time asking myself what each word represented. After much writing, I realized that I was drawn to a deeper meaning of each word.

Pioneer became innovation, creative thinking, inspiration, seeing things differently. Letting go of boundaries and Exploring the unknown, seeing beyond the horizon, building bridges for those that follow.

Honest became genuine, truthful, loyal and steadfast, forthright and trustworthy. Caring became idealistic, wanting the best for everyone, collaboration, coordination, uplifting, teaching, encouraging and facilitating change. I discovered a part of me I never knew existed.

As I gained a better understanding of myself it was easier to do more of what I love to do. I began drawing and painting after an absence of 35 years. I added color to my accounting work; creating checklist and control sheet in colors. I began writing. This was a tremendous change because I lean more toward numbers than writing. I discovered that I am talented and know a lot about bookkeeping and operations management. I began to embrace my inner business expert. I was asked to be a featured expert and write articles for a women's magazine.

I began to believe in myself. I started to know that I am important and a worthwhile and contributing person. It is ok to occupy my own space. I now keep a notebook by my bed and write out my thoughts when things are troubling me or if I get stuck in a loop worrying or feeling confused. My main "go to" defense was to be in confusion. Like a deer in headlights, I would become immobilized. I could not think or find solutions. Sometimes I could not even name the problem or issue. I would call a friend and she would remind me to breathe. Pause and breathe.

I have tools today to help when I feel stuck, confused or overwhelmed because of all the work I had done around finding myself. I've discovered it's important to have these tools when I get immobilized. The key is to be able to find your way to get yourself back on track. I would like to share some of the tools I use to see if they may be tools that could help you too.

1. **Meditate and ground yourself.** Meditate and ground yourself in the present moment. Start by touching the floor with the palms of both hands and then sit down. Imagine your feet grounded into the earth and imagine your ancestors and guides down in the earth sending up healing power through you. Visualize that you are receiving all the help you need from the center of the earth.

2. **Write.** Write in the morning. I quickly writing out all my thoughts in a continuous flow until everything is out at that moment. I am analytical, so I tend to overthink things. You may express your feelings in a different way and that is fine.

3. **Be in nature.** Feel the grass or sand beneath your feet. Maybe water brings you peace or the flow of a babbling brook or raging river or the calm stillness of a deep pool of water.

4. **Exercise and Movement.** You may find physical exercise, running or working out to be your stabilizing force.

5. **Get Support.** Remember life is not a solo journey. We don't have to do everything on our own and in fact it is much richer when we let others walk beside us.

6. **Find Your Spark.** Make sure to include some fun in your day; something you love that fills you up. Like, I started painting again. Find the things that lift you up.

7. **Be consistent.** Include these steps in your life daily. You are worth it and I want you to have joy and that spark in your life on a daily basis.

Whatever it is, do what feels right for you. Find a way to stay in touch with your innermost feelings. Doing this routinely will make a huge difference in your life.

Trust the process even if it feels like what you are doing right now does not directly affect your business or income. As you add stability and clarity you will gain a different outlook on life. Challenges may even become opportunities for growth, enhancements, and improvements.

I have reached a place where I now see where all things are for my good. I am not perfect. That is not what we are here to accomplish. I do believe we are here to be seen and heard. And that each level of expansion has its own "wonderfulness" build into the experience. We just need to step back and see it.

I invite you to work with any of the many holistic healer and coaches to find your own way to feed your inner self. I have experienced amazing revelations during guided meditations with many of the healers in my area.

It may not seem like this has anything to do with business but as you feel more confident and capable within yourself, internally things will shift and change on the outside too. As I gained clarity I was able to be ready for the job of my dreams when it presented itself.

Today, my spark shows up in my life in little ways and big ways every day. For example, I name every workday of the week. I work daily with my biggest client, so my first e-mail of the day closes with the name I make up for that day.

I may close with Happy Magnificent Monday. I use a word that matches the Day of the Week. Finance Fridays, Tremendous Tuesdays, and Wonderful Wednesdays. It changes with my mood but always positive even when we were sick, it was Wellness Wednesday and when it was cold Wintery Wednesday or in frustration Wacky Wednesday or We Can Do This Wednesday. I have fun with setting the pace for the day and it lifts others up too.

I have noticed that when I add innovative ways of doing regular activities I am able to add a spark to those activities. Even if it is just adding colors to a column in the checklist or write the list on bright colored paper. I find a way add fun to the task at hand, increasing my motivation and engagement with getting the work done.

This is also directly related to what I have discovered about my unique approach to things. Referring back to this list of how I think and using those values adds a spark to get things done as well.

Find your "Spark." The bright energy that recharges you kindles your spirit and activates your purpose.

1. Find things that are easy to add to your routine.
2. Do more. Not only by yourself but with help leverage and delegate. Never abdicate.
3. Go easy on yourself, remember to breathe and meditate or have quiet moments to yourself.

You already possess everything you need to be successful. Believe in yourself.

Celebrate wins – especially those small ones you tend to think don't matter. They give you momentum. They are proof of your achievement. I am all for momentum, keep doing things and do more,

Give yourself permission to be your bigger self, go beyond thriving, allow yourself to flourish!

I can now see how everything I have done and experienced, both good and challenges, have helped me to embrace my bigger self. Truly knowing and understanding myself has given me much joy, peace and ability to keep going.

Life is good today. I am truly happy that I have found my way to step forward and shine. When I am being innovative, creative, inspirational, steadfast, collaborative, uplifting and facilitating change and improvement it makes a decisive difference in my ability to work with ease.

Where is your version of Pioneer, Honest and Caring? Now go out and identify your values. And, more importantly, flip the switch.

About the Author

Gayle Bode began her fascination of the small business financial process when she was 8 years old. She loved to look down from the 2nd story windows of their upstairs office and observe how her family's medium size grocery store functioned - from stocking the shelves, to shopping carts being filled with goods, to checking out at the register. Everything was neatly in its place and every location had a function. The freezers kept the frozen food frozen while the fresh produce was up front near the windows for all to see, inviting them to come in. There was order and creativity to the placement of everything. Gayle dreamed of having her own business one day, a very specific type of business - specializing in bookkeeping, accounting and operations management.

Gayle fulfilled that dream when she became the Owner of Bode Office Solutions providing Office Management and Bookkeeping Services in 2009. She has worked in the areas of Office Management, Administrative and Operational Management for CPA firms, Dental & Chiropractic Offices for over 28 years. Gayle helps business owners get more comfortable with their day to day Money IN and Money OUT relationship and have a more realistic conversation around their money without judgment or fear. Gayle specializes in working with holistic healers, auto shops, therapists, architects and engineers.

Gayle Bode has actively established an experiential lifestyle for herself and her family of overcoming challenges and setbacks and doing more on a regular basis. Gayle makes mental and emotional health a priority while maintaining a sense of curiosity, learning and teaching.

To find out more about Gayle you can go to her website at www.bodeoffice.com.

Email Address: gayle@bodeoffice.com

Phone Number 925-270-5458

Facebook - https://www.facebook.com/gayle.bode

Soul Whispers: A Deep Inner Journey
Jena Harris

Have you ever felt the powerful soul whispers from God that penetrates you to your core? Or the soft soul whispers that comes from deep within, leading you to answers that you knew all along? These whispers can be heard when you are still and felt when you are open to receive. Let's go on this journey within together soul sister.

Shhhh…. Do you hear it?

It's faint, yet powerful.

It's the benevolent whisper of God.

Come with me and you will see just how much I love you, whispers God.
You have to trust me even when you don't see the road ahead.
But God, she said, why is this so journey hard?
I have been left in the dirt and left very scarred.
You say you love me, yet I endured such neglect.
Where were you then God? Not with me is what I suspect.
I made my way to adulthood and found the love of my life,
As I poured out my love only to feel such strife.
Why did you leave me then God?
You left me abroad.
I birthed a child that you took too early as you say that you care.
All of those nights alone, as I lay in prayer.

How could you leave me at the times I needed you most?
Dear child, I never left you, you left me.
Do you remember? Oh how you forget, you see.
The woman that you saved from her death and despair.
Because of your journey, and what with her you shared.
She learned through your eyes to not choose that path to take,
Instead of your blessing you see the heartache.
Do you see your life is full of purpose and love?
Always connected to the heavens above.
Don't you see, because of your abuse she did not suffer,
It was because your choice to be the buffer.
Because of your experience, you chose another way,
What you don't realize is that it led you to astray.
Do you remember that time you made the near miss,
It was then that I saved you from the traumatic abyss.
So as you feel the frustration with me,
I have never left your side don't you see.
The cross that you have carried may be bigger than most,
Yet you had the help of the Holy Ghost.
When comparing to other's and stepping in their shoes,
It comes down to the perspective you choose.
I love you, and I will never leave you.
You sometimes forget and overcomplicate what is true,
I gave you everything you will ever need inside of you,
It really is simple, it all comes back to love.

Shhhhh…..Be still.
If you listen you will hear.
She is your inner super girl.

Soul whispers,

You are more than what you believe. Do you remember WHO YOU ARE?

Your childlike spirit is unblemished; No judgment or bias, fearless and open to all possibilities with a presence of wonder, and unquenchable curiosity.

Do you remember laughing for no reason?

Do you remember playing until dark and riding your bike until your parents called you in?

Do you remember being so proud of the first time you tied your shoes and your first cartwheel on the lawn?

You didn't worry about how your hair looked, as you loved your uncombed hair and missing front teeth.

Do you remember? Have you forgotten?

Life is to be explored, discovering what makes you happy.

Do you remember how special you are?

Shhhhh..... Be still and smile.

She's here within, you just forgot.

Let's go deep.

Within your soul is a brave little super girl who lives within your wonder woman outer shell. She is there to guide you with child-like energy and whispers words of wisdom that can only come through the innocent eyes of a child. If you listen closely she will remind you of your boundless bravery that you may have left behind, and your simplistic, yet beautifully perfect character that is still within.

Your inner super girl whispers are your reminder of how to live.

You have a lifetime of visions and impressions from your heart that began as a child. The visions were vivid and bright, and over time may have turned to black and white. Your dreams may have been forgotten, lost, or covered up from the layers of our world. Don't forget soul sister, that **this life is your canvas. A canvas to paint, to explore, and to create into your magical work of art filled with laughter, joy, excitement, sadness, heartache, pain and everything in between. You are given a fresh start** each day, and sometimes that may mean that you give yourself a clean canvas too.

Don't be afraid to re-create yourself no matter what your age is, no matter what you have done in your past, no matter where your journey may have led you. Don't let go of the dreams that you once imagined, even if they may not have manifested how you envisioned, know that all is well.

Close your eyes and sit back to embrace your inner calm and stillness. I invite you to see a possibility that everything is as it should be. The experiences in your beautiful journey have all molded you into who you are today. Be so proud of that soul sister, for you have been delicately and beautifully created. Every single cell in your body, every hair on your head, you are perfectly imperfect and exactly what the world needs.

Soul whispers,

You are so loved just as you are.

Your mistakes don't define you.

YOU KNOW WHO YOU ARE.....

Let's connect to your wisdom.

Take a deep breath. Do you feel it? Your soul is reminding you of God's unconditional love and your unshakable strength that you may have forgotten about. It's always there for you and will never leave you. Close your eyes, place your hands over your heart, and re-connect to your breath.

I've discovered your inner spiritual path is connected to your inner whisper. And this is your individual journey, and yours alone. Others can walk the path with you, but no one can walk it for you. As I have been on my own personal journey, I have come to realize that I don't fit in any kind of box in any area of my life, especially when it comes to religion. And that is ok, as I have given myself permission to step out of the box. It's helped me connect to my own self-love, self-acceptance, and my voice for how I connect to God. God within.

I'm so very grateful that my mom did not pressure my sisters and I to believe a certain way.

She wanted us to discover this on our own, and create our own private connection to God. I have been blessed in my life to not only study but to experience many different religious beliefs, experiences and perspectives. There seemed to be an underlying and resonating truth in most of the religions practices. And what I mean by this is they were all saying the same thing, just saying it a bit differently. It's called Love. I call it choosing love. I am so grateful for this diversity as it has led me to my belief, and my core truth. That love is my religion, and that I have God flowing within me, and I can access the love, the wisdom, and the truth by closing my eyes and taking a deep breath to hear to the whispers.

Soul whispers,

Boldly be who God created you to be and you will illuminate and inspire the world around you.

To be able to say I chose love as my religion, took me many years of ups and downs, self-growth, self-acceptance, self-love, and spiritual maturing. As I healed my wounds, I began to peel the layers away and also attuned my senses to hear the soul whispers that I had once heard as a child. I don't remember exactly when the soul whispers faded away, but I do remember when I reconnected to them. It is my belief that these whispers are available to each one of us, if the person is open to hearing and receiving to them. I hope you are inspired to connect to yourself in a deeper, more intimate way.

'One of the biggest setbacks of our life is when we listen to the wrong whispers. The ones that limit us and keep us feeling small.'

~Jena Harris

Here are 5 simple steps to connect to your soul whispers.

1. Close your eyes, place your hands over your heart, and take a few long and slow deep breaths.
2. Accept yourself completely.
3. Remember that you are not your thoughts.
4. Allow yourself to feel what you feel and connect how you connect.
5. Take your time and let your soul guide you.

I want to stimulate your mind with a simple thought, although this is my perspective, I hope to infuse more light in your journey and so that you never feel alone. The simple thought is that there is no right or wrong way in the course to God when you chose the path of love. Love is the final answer, in all that you seek. Love will lighten even the darkest hatred, love will heal the deepest pain, and love will comfort the loneliest soul even if they are in bitterness. Love is the strength that feeds and nurtures our deep innate desire of wanting to be accepted and loved.

At the source of the world's struggle, it's seeking to fill a hole. A hole that is a longing for a deeper connection to God and ourselves. It is also my belief that we can attain this connection through love. Through this deep self-journey, love bridges the gap between mankind, and mother earth.

This powerful energy that is fed directly to the one source that unites us all together, *GOD*.

It doesn't matter what your choice for the path to get to God, as long as the path is walking through love. To love one another. Love is God. God is love. Therefore, in my opinion, love is the universal religion. And within each beat of our hearts, deep within the human body and heart lies the whispers of our soul that are connected through love. And if we listen intently we can hear the soft soul whispers that are there for each one of us.

We often as humans can tend to overcomplicate the truth. It is always about love. It is always about experiencing, expanding, giving, and receiving love. We always come back to love. We entered into this world from love and we leave and go to love.

Soul whispers,
You are not lost, you have just forgotten.

I do believe I will always be in a state of continuous growing, learning, and expanding in my own inner soul journey. I also believe we are here to experience all that is. This is the ups and the downs, the ebbs and the flows of our human journey. The multi-dimensional layers, the flavors of life choices, and the directions of a soul's path through free will are all here to sculpt you into an even more beautiful version of who you already are; Like a flower in a tight bud that just keeps opening and expanding in the most glorious way.

A deep soul journey is a quest in which we set out to discover a deeper meaning of self-love and acceptance; a deeper dive into who we truly are and the purpose of it all.

My prayer for you is that you dare enough to keep running when you feel like stopping, or when quitting feels like the easier thing to do. May you feel the courage and strength to look up when the world is teaching you to look down. May the light illuminate your truth of authenticity to shine forward in all that you do as you follow the guidance of your soul whisper. Keep walking forward with your head high looking up. Because you are perfect and exactly what the world needs, just as God made you.

…And while you are listening, reconnecting to your soul, and remembering that you are so loved, remember that I love you.

"Life isn't about finding yourself, it's about connecting, remembering, and co-creating what is already inside."
~Jena Harris

About the Author

Jena is a spiritual transformation teacher, energetic healing facilitator, and bestselling author. She is the founder of Sisterhood Connections, where she loves to connect, empower, and inspire her tribe of women from all around the world. She holds a Master's in Arts and Metaphysical Studies and spent twenty-two years in Corporate America, working around the U.S. In 2009 she started her healing business Blissfully Empowered and then in 2013 founded and started Sisterhood Connections. In 2014 she left her corporate position to pursue her dreams of connecting soul sisters for a 'new kind of sisterhood' and assisting sisters and brothers to deliberately create their purpose driven life & business.

Jena is also the author of three published books, the bestselling **"Who Were You Before The World Told You Who To Be", "44 Days Returning To Love"** and **"Manifest Your Power Partner".** Jena is a Reiki Master and a skilled expert in homeopathic modalities of human healing and wellness with studies in Christ centered healing, matrix energetics, healing touch and metaphysical studies.

She assists sisters and brothers across the world connect to their authenticity and who they were before the world told them who to be, teaching them exactly how they were created is exactly what the world needs.

Email Address: jena@sisterhoodconnections.org

Phone Number: 208-860-0411

Website: https://www.jenaharris.com

Facebook: https://www.facebook.com/blissfullyempowered/

LinkedIn: https://www.linkedin.com/in/jena-harris-786a86a6/

Twitter: https://twitter.com/BEmpoweredLife

YouTube: https://www.youtube.com/channel/UCW7LmXXD8WKtY_CD9VgaVPw

Instagram: https://www.instagram.com/jenaharris_/

Financially Step Forward and SHINE
Everybody has a gift! What's yours?
Marlene Elizabeth, M.Ed.

I sit quietly at the local Honda dealership early one weekday morning, waiting for an oil change service, as gentle Christmas music plays softly throughout the lobby. Suddenly, a bright, booming, friendly voice enters the room. I look up from my laptop and spot a well-dressed customer sporting a handsome black suit, polished shoes and a wide, happy-go-lucky grin. With a grand entrance, he positions himself in front of the sleepy crowd of service-guests watching morning news and boldly announces: *"all those who would like to take me out to breakfast, please remain seated!"*

Ha! His "out-of-the-box," gutsy humor creates laughter in the room, tickles my funny bone, and immediately brightens my day.

In the midst of holiday light and presents, this gentleman's obvious extroverted nature and authentic talent for making people laugh instantly reminds me of a powerful and clear insight I've learned in my work as a money coach for women:

An essential key for creating a healthy relationship to money involves having tender clarity of your natural strengths, talents and sharing those gifts in service to others.

Knowing this is just one of the many reasons I love my work! I have the honor and pleasure of helping women uncover their hidden gifts and natural strengths, as part of their process of creating a healthier relationship to money. This is the work I am called and gifted to do.

The Challenge of Thriving In Our Talents And Strengths

I was a fourth grader when I participated in my first and only audition for the lead role of Nancy in the school musical Oliver Jr. I don't recall if my parents knew about it, only that it was an opportunity I wanted to try and jumped at the chance. I made it to the final round, without any voice training whatsoever, competing against a sixth grader who took private voice lessons. Although she won the role, I felt grateful and encouraged that I'd made it that far on my own, natural ability. Decades later, however, after reading the note my music teacher had written in my report card that year "*Marlene would benefit from private music lessons*", I realized for the first time, that she probably didn't "just write that in everyone's report card" as I believed all those years. It was the first time I recognized **that we can have talents hidden inside us that we never knew existed**; or if we did, were never nurtured or cultivated during childhood.

Today, one of my super powers is to help women discover, nurture and cultivate their hidden gifts and talents so they can financially step forward and shine in a powerful way! The secret ingredient behind this superpower is my undying belief in her potential and possibilities, coupled with my expertise as a certified brain personality specialist. My clients receive custom brain personality assessments based on the latest research in neuroscience. Each report reveals the client's native Communication Style / Sensory preference (auditory, visual or kinesthetic); Introversion / Extroversion ratio; Brain Strengths and Personality Type and an in-depth look at female/male brain differences that cause each gender to have different perspectives and different ways of processing information.

(Couples also benefit greatly from this coaching!)

I know without a doubt that all of us are born with rich, unique and natural strengths, gifts and talents created on purpose, for us to share in this life.

Unfortunately, the tragic poverty of this reality is that these treasures, our gifts, far too often remain buried deep inside of us, never seeing the light of day.

Sadly, our silent, unchallenged fears, doubts and shame can repeatedly prevent us from financially stepping forward and shining. Sometimes, we become so internally disconnected from our gifts, we're not even aware they exist. Year after year, our untapped potential slowly begins to erode our confidence, self-esteem, sense of purpose, direction, fulfillment, and prosperity. Over time as this continues, we're left with a sense of meaninglessness, frustration, and dwindled-hope. We can't understand how we got to this place that's so far from the life of our dreams. ***"What happened?"*** we ask ourselves in desperation. As this happens, our relationships, jobs, bank accounts and health tend to also suffer. All of this robs us from enjoying the personal and financial freedom we were meant to live.

As motivational speaker Les Brown powerfully illuminates: "The graveyard is the richest place on earth, because it is here that you will find all the hopes and dreams that were never fulfilled, the books that were never written, the songs that were never sung, the inventions that were never shared, the cures that were never discovered, all because someone was too afraid to take that first step, keep with the problem, or (remain) determined to carry out their dream."

Far too many individuals experience the pain of this suffering needlessly. It's time to create new personal money stories and build new family legacies!

When we are supported and encouraged to share our love and natural gifts in the world, we not only experience the abundant life we were meant to live, but in the process, also become the gift of joy and peace our family, friends and world deserve to experience, too.

Defining True 'Success' and 'Wealth'

Success certainly means different things to different people. John C. Maxwell beautifully and simply captures the way I view it. Mr. Maxwell defines success as ***"knowing your purpose in life, growing to meet your maximum potential and sowing seeds that benefit others."*** How do you define success?

One of my favorite money stories is about a determined woman who turned her love for cookies into a $450 million-dollar empire. Of course, most of us would relish having such an extraordinary sum of money, especially doing what we love! Her financial success is awe-inspiring. Yet what deeply moves me beyond the money she created is the extraordinary *choice* 'Debbi Fields,' founder of Mrs. Fields, made during a painful - and pivotal- life experience.

During dinner one night, at the beautiful, but intimidating home of one of her husband's clients, the man asked her "What do you do?" "Oh," she replied, "I'm just trying to get orientated." The man got up, pulled an enormous, leather-bound dictionary off the shelf, put it in her lap and said, "The word is *oriented*. If you can't speak the English language, you shouldn't speak at all."

Incredibly embarrassed, Debbi Fields sat there in his library with tears streaming down her cheeks. The man's shaming words and actions hurt terribly. In that moment, she could have let doubt reign and allow herself to remain feeling small and insignificant. Instead, she heard her father's voice, who taught her that **true wealth is found in family, friends and doing what you love.** That night, she gathered herself together and set out to live her purpose, grow to meet her maximum potential and sow seeds that benefit others. With the internal, emotionally healthy, landscape she inherited from her family, she chose to love, trust her gifts and believe in herself. The wealth she manifested on the outside reflects the wealth she already owned on the inside - a beautiful example of financial self-care that touches me every time I remember her story.

Sharing Our Gifts In Service To Others

Mrs. Fields loved cookies. For me, I love to sing and dance. What do you love doing?

My brain is naturally wired to engage primarily with the world kinesthetically, as opposed to in an auditory or visual fashion. This means that my brain processes information most efficiently and effectively based on what I *feel* (e.g., touch or feel in my gut).

Yet, by age 8, I learned it was *not* safe to interact with my world kinesthetically and subconsciously shut down this vital way for me of being in the world. Without knowing it, I became disconnected from the rich sensory world around me that gives me strength. Instead of thriving in my unique design, with my natural desire to grow, expand and explore, shame silently slid into the driver's seat of my life, keeping my world much smaller than I was ever meant to experience it.

It wasn't until I was twenty-eight years old, during graduate school when I suddenly experienced a powerful awakening. I've always loved dance but never took it seriously as a career path or even pursued it as a hobby. During my studies at Boston College, however, I had the opportunity to stretch beyond my comfort zone and enrolled in an elective Liturgical Dance class. Although I felt completely like a fish out of water, I relished the experience of learning body movements to spiritual music. One of our assignments was to choreograph our own movements to a musical arrangement. I was not surprised that I found the homework easy to complete and performed it fairly confidently the next day in class. What did surprise me is what happened next. During the final class, our professor displayed a video-taped presentation of our individual, choreographed performances. After watching several students perform their pieces, a dancer appeared on the screen that I did not recognize.

She was such a *natural*, so graceful and beautiful, I didn't remember seeing her in class. I asked, "Who's that?" The students and professor quickly replied, "That's you Marlene!" It was obvious to everyone who had seen that dancer, except to me. For several seconds, I sat there stunned (and slightly embarrassed for not recognizing my own self). **I simply could not believe it was *me*.** For one brief moment in time, I felt like a stranger to myself, completely disconnected from ever **realizing that potential lived within me... until the experience of witnessing myself with fresh eyes.**

Have you ever felt like a stranger to yourself when you 'accidentally' discovered a natural talent you never knew existed inside of you; one that fits you like a glove, one that gives you deep joy?

Today, I integrate my kinesthetic gifts, my love of song and dance, creatively into my work as a certified money coach. Helping clients *feel and experience* a healthier relationship to money is what I enjoy most, do best and sets me apart in the marketplace as a mamapreneur. I love providing clients with a safe retreat-like setting where they can engage their senses around money conversations with "body-check in's" (a simple, yet profound practice I learned from financial therapist Bari Tessler), scented candles, fresh flowers and nibbles of dark chocolate while we explore the deep terrain of my clients' money stories, challenges and new beginnings.

You Are Called and Gifted To Financially Shine!

Please enjoy the following tips and strategies that you can implement immediately to help you shine financially:

1. **Uncover Your Hidden Strengths!** Step into your power by completing a Brain Personality Mini Quiz at www.brainhappylife.com (free tool to support you!)

2. **Discover Your Money Type!** Learn about the 8 Money Types and take the Money Type. Quiz at www.growmoneywings.com (free tool to support you!)

3. **Ease Money Stress With Financial Self-care.** Create financial mini-spa dates for yourself. Doing so can help cultivate a sense of trust, safety and well-being in your relationship to money. Infuse your space with scented candles, fresh flowers, a favorite beverage, relaxing music, cozy slippers, nibbles of dark chocolate. *Inhale.* Exhale deeply. Handle challenging money interactions, one brave feather at a time with mega doses of self-compassion. What clues is your body sharing with you physically, emotionally, mentally and spiritually, as related to your finances? Listen and

honor your body's wisdom. Seek encouragement and support, as necessary.

4. **Grow MoneyWings!** For inspiration, listen to *Break The Shell* (sung by India Arie). Read money books (I share some of my personal favorites on my website). Find a money conversation cafe or money coaching circle in person or online (for more details on both of these events I offer, please visit my website). Value and honor the natural gifts you've been given to share.

5. **Take action now.** Don't wait until someday, you deserve to financially shine now!

If you're ready to start unfolding your personal and financial potential, I'd love to offer you a private **45-minute complimentary, one-on-one money coaching session** where you'll receive compassionate, creative, personalized strategies to support your dreams and goals.

To book your private session with Marlene, please visit www.meetwithmarlene.com.

About the Author

Marlene Elizabeth is an Author, Speaker, Mamapreneur and Certified Money Coach®.

Deeply inspired by her financial dream to raise a money-smart girl as a single stay-at-home Mom, Marlene released her bestselling book *MONEYWINGS*™ on her daughter's 11th birthday. For years, Marlene questioned *"why do financial dreams seem so easy for others to achieve, but not for me?"* As a financial-role model for her daughter, it became her mission to find the answer by living the question. Her book is a Spirit-filled love-note to help women kindle their confidence in their relationship to money, and ultimately in themselves.

Marlene believes the world needs the financial dream in every woman's heart to come true. Her deeply caring, collaborative leadership style empowers her audiences and clients to embrace financial self-care. Women learn life-changing strategies to breakthrough limiting money beliefs so they can uncover their unique, untapped financial potential. They discover their authentic gifts and strengths while developing a powerful sense of confidence, clarity and purpose to thrive.

Marlene's weekly podcast *"Let's Get Tender™: Money Conversations That Matter"* (RHG-TV Network) empowers women to see money differently so they can stop doubting and start unfolding their financial dream one brave feather at a time.

Her next book *"Embrace Your Wealth: Living A Financially Spiritual Life is due for release"* April 2019. She is a featured contributing author in *"Bloom Where You Are Planted and SHINE!," Empowering YOU, Transforming Lives"* 365 Daily Reflections (available December 2018) and *"Step Into Your Brilliance"* (available Fall 2019).

Marlene earned her Master's degree in Religious Education from Boston College School of Theology and Ministry and B.A. in International Relations from U.C. Davis. She is also a Certified Brain Personality Specialist.

Marlene would love to hear from you!
e: marlene@marleneelizabeth.com
p: 909.247.1127
w: www.marleneelizabeth.com
f: www.facebook.com/growmoneywings

SECTION TWO

ALIGN WITH YOUR PURPOSE

Discover how to align fully with your purpose. Be inspired to align your values and life to be on purpose with those things that matter most to you.

Follow Your Heart and SHINE
Nancy Monson, MA, MBA, CPCC

Standing in front of the audience, I suddenly realize that I've finally overcome my fear and shame of performing. I'm both excited and scared, but deep inside I feel elated. Everyone is looking expectantly at me. Now it's my turn to shine!

I share where it all began, in front of the audience I become myself at 6 years old...helping them see, feel and understand through my little girl eyes...

> *It's Christmas! I'm 6 years old. All my brothers and sisters and nieces and nephews are here! I love it when everyone comes to visit.*
>
> *There's my daddy! He's got the movie camera with the big fancy lights! I love it when he takes pictures! I love to be in the pictures. I dance, make funny faces and pose for the camera. I'm so excited!*
>
> *Uh! Oh, there's my mommy...*
>
> *"Nancy Lynn, get over here! You're embarrassing me!" She shoves me out of the living room and into the bedroom. I trip, fall and hit my face on the bedframe. It hurts and I start to cry. I get up and look in the mirror. My eye is already turning black from hitting the bedframe. "I'm sorry mommy. It's my fault. I'll be good. I'll be quiet." I slink quietly back into the corner of the living room, hoping no one will notice me and my painful black eye.*

My performance is the culmination of two months of storytelling training where I learned how to powerfully and captivatingly tell my story using improvisational theatre techniques. My heart was very clear that I was to sign up for the class even though it meant driving 2 hours each way to attend the sessions. My mind thought I was crazy and tried hard to convince me this was not a good decision. Fortunately, on this occasion, I trusted the clear "yes" that my heart shouted to me. When I signed up, I had no idea that it would be a life transforming experience, reconnecting me with painful childhood experiences buried in my memory. Through reconnecting, I let go and embodied more of who I truly am designed to be.

I continue my performance with what happened a few months later...

> *I'm at school. It's lunchtime and the whole school is in the lunchroom eating. I'm sitting at a small table with my girlfriends. We're laughing and goofing around. The teacher sees us and bellows, "Nancy Cranfill, you're making too much noise. Go sit on the counter and be quiet!" I'm horrified and embarrassed. Slowly I get up and, with my head down, walk over to sit up on the counter while everyone in the lunchroom watches me. I swallow my tears and sit there without looking at anyone until I'm dismissed after they've all gone out to play.*

My performance was a huge success, and more importantly, I had a blast! People from the audience congratulated me, saying they loved watching me. They shared with me their painful stories from childhood. Many, including the course instructor, told me I have a gift for performing. I was stunned and humbled by their responses. In my mind, I never knew that about myself, but clearly my heart knew.

Have you ever had moments that left a mark or imprint of fear in you? Causing you to shrink back rather than shine? If so, I want you to know you can move through the fear and step into who you are truly meant and made to be with joy, wonder and excitement.

From these two terribly painful experiences I shut down my bubbly, boisterous and enthusiastic little girl that loved to perform. A year later, I spent five terrifying days in the hospital with bronchial pneumonia, and every year after until I was in my late 20s I either contracted bronchitis or laryngitis. I literally shut down my voice.

My emotional wounding went deep, and even though, as an adult, I have led hundreds of workshops, given dozens of talks and keynote speeches, **I have never had the courage to step out of the lecturer role and truly perform—be that bubbly, engaging little girl who loved an audience. It wasn't until I reconnected with my 6-year old, buried deep inside my heart, that I found the courage to let her step forward and shine**

again. Through that experience, I reconnected with one of my essential gifts I kept locked away for fear of shame and embarrassment.

My path of personal awakening didn't start with the storytelling course. I've been on a personal growth journey for decades. However, that course **was the key to unlocking what I had yet to fully implement in my life. My heart was clear, and this time I listened. I will never let that little girl hide in the shadows again.** Her gift of performing is one of my natural talents that I am meant to embody and shine in my life.

Through my journey of reclaiming my gifts and talents, I learned three keys that helped me step forward and shine. I share these keys with you in the hopes that they will help you embrace your talents, banish your fears, and help you step forward and shine!

Key Number 1: Trust your unique inner guidance—your "built in" decision-making—and follow your heart! We each have inner guidance that, when we follow it, helps us live our most fulfilling life. My heart was clearly telling me to register for the storytelling workshop, but my head was telling me it was crazy. Like many of my decisions, it wanted me to evaluate all the reasons why I should or shouldn't do it. More often than naught, I would end up choosing the "rational" option instead of my heart's guidance. **On the occasion that I would follow my heart, it always led to the best, most amazing and fulfilling outcomes.**

You too likely have made decisions that led to wondrous fulfillment and decisions that didn't turn out well. To help you get clear with how you're designed to make your best decisions, I offer the following reflection:

- *Think of when you made one of the best decisions of your life: What was your process? How is that process similar to your other good decisions? What keeps you from following that process consistently?*

Key Number 2: Recognize and embrace your natural talents and gifts. I hid my bubbly little girl because I believed she was not wanted, discounting my natural gift of performing. That experience taught me that I frequently discount the things that are easy and effortless for me either because of negative feedback or because I thought it was nothing special. I assumed it was easy for everyone. I believed I had to "work hard" at being talented or good enough. **Living this way made my life far more difficult than it could have been if I had recognized and fostered those things I naturally do well, almost without trying.**

Many of us are encouraged to take a reasonable path in life, one that "guarantees" success and financial security. For several years I taught a women's leadership development program. Almost all the women who attended were between the ages of 25 and 35. They had been working for a few years after completing college, but now were looking for a more fulfilling career. They had followed the course either their parents or their counselors recommended, turning a deaf ear to their inner guidance and discounting their natural talents. They took my program because they were not willing to continue to deny their hearts' calling.

It's time to reclaim and celebrate your natural talents and gifts—the abilities you were born to embody and cultivate. Take time to reflect on the following questions:

- *What comes so naturally to you that you discount your ability? What did you love to do as a child that you stuffed because of negative conditioning? How can you recognize, cultivate and fully embody your natural talents and gifts?*

Key Number 3: Banish your conditioning that keeps you from fully embodying your gifts and talents. Your self-criticism and self-judgment are conditioning that keeps you from living your best self—the life you are meant to live. Ever since those painful experiences from my childhood I've had a vicious inner critic that kept me from embracing my talent for performing because it was not welcomed. My inner critic's job was to keep me from ever putting myself in a situation where I would be shamed for not acting appropriately, which led me to chronically overachieve. I had to be the best or I would avoid putting myself in a situation where my internalized critic would rake me over the coals.

My inner critic was so ruthless and overpowering that it almost cost me my life. It pushed me to such extremes that I developed anxiety and depression from a demanding job that was not aligned at all with my natural abilities. It drove me to be the best at everything I did, no matter whether it was effortless or arduous. It exhausted me to the point of mental illness from the constant fear that I was never good enough.

While it's good to try hard and do your best, it's not healthy to be driven to point of harming yourself or keeping your natural talents buried. We all have self-judgment and self-criticism that keep us from bringing out our true talents, robbing us of the joy and fulfillment we are meant to experience. Take a moment to reflect on these questions to help you recognize your conditioning:

- *When do you experience the most self-criticism or self-judgment? How does it hold you back from bringing out your innate gifts or from living the life you dream of?*

If you've taken the time to answer the previous questions, you now have more clarity about:

- How you are designed to make your best decisions
- Your natural gifts and talents
- What's holding you back from fully expressing your gifts and talents

Armed with this clarity and if you are ready to step forward and shine, I have a few suggestions for next steps:

- **Trust your inner decision-making process and follow your guidance.** Now that you are aware of how to make your best decisions, start to tune in and use that process for making decisions. To practice, start with small decisions that have low consequences. Experiment to see how it goes. What results are you getting? What are you learning about your process?

- **Claim your natural talents and gifts.** Find opportunities to bring out at least one of the talents you know you have but are not fully embodying. Play with this talent and see what happens. If you have difficulty recognizing your natural talents, pick a few trusted friends or family members to ask them what talents they see in you.

- **Personify your inner critic.** What does it look like? If it had a name, what would it be? Be playful with it and use your imagination. When I did this exercise, I knew instantly what my critic looked like—a giant, hairy, knuckle-dragging ogre with big sharp teeth that drooled! Get a toy that represents your inner critic. When it starts to terrorize you, take your toy and put it in a drawer. Throw it in the trash or put it outside. Have fun when dealing with your critic. Inner critics are NEVER playful. I tell my critic to "go play on the freeway!" The key is to personify your critic, get it out of your head and break the pattern of it controlling your mindset.

If you would like assistance identifying your decision-making process, pinpointing your talents or recognizing your conditioning, I can help. I personally know how scary and difficult that journey can be. Making my way through my emotional wounds and conditioning to recognize and embody how I am designed to be led me to the work I do today. I am committed to helping you banish your inner critic and be who you are meant to be! This is what I do for my clients. Utilizing the *Human Design* and *Gene Keys Systems*, I reveal your unique decision-making, talents and gifts, and help you eliminate what is keeping you from stepping forward and shining. Use the link in my bio to apply for my complimentary *Unlock Your Design Session*. I would be delighted to help you step forward and shine the beautiful you that you were born to be.

About the Author

Nancy Monson, MA, MBA, CPCC is a Soul Purpose Advocate devoted to helping people live their soul's greatest expression every day. She brings a multitude of skills, talents, wisdom and a lifetime of transformative experiences to guide people who are truly ready to live their soul's potential and purpose every day.

Working in both corporate consulting and personal transformation for the past twenty years, Nancy has a unique combination of experience helping hundreds of senior leaders, executive teams, and entrepreneurs using her unique combination of strategic, intuitive and pragmatic skills. This experience gives her a special ability to mentor women leaders and entrepreneurs as they struggle to navigate their own personal transformations. Her greatest fulfillment comes from confidently guiding women dealing with difficult and challenging life changes to create truly powerful, authentic soul-directed lives.

Nancy holds an MBA in Organizational Behavior from UC Berkeley's Hass School of Business, an MA in the Science of Creative Intelligence from the Maharishi University of Management, and a BS in Mathematics from Cal Poly, San Luis Obispo. She also has completed numerous trainings with special emphasis in Human Design, Gene Keys, Evolutionary Leadership, life and relationship coaching, spiritual guidance, Tantric counseling, Deep Emotional Release™ bodywork, and Reiki energy healing. Nancy is also a facilitator of 7 Habits of Highly Effective People personal empowerment course and a coach of the Women, Power, and Body Esteem transformation program for women.

Nancy is also an adventurer. She treasures the outdoors, and spends as much time as she can hiking the hills around her California home. In her years of travel and outdoor adventure, she has hiked the Sierra Nevada, the Cascades, Andes, Himalayas, Alaska Range, Brooks Range, and the Rockies. She has backpacked one range or another during every season of the year, climbed frozen waterfalls, numerous rock faces and mountains, and camped on snowy glaciers. Her greatest accomplishment was climbing Denali, the highest peak in North America at the time when it was uncommon to see women in such sports. She believes nature is immensely healing and transformative, taking us to a deep place of inner connection with our own true nature.

nancy@nancymonsoncoaching.com

209.217.8120

www.nancylynnmonson.com

https://www.facebook.com/nlmonson

https://www.linkedin.com/in/nancymonson

https://twitter.com/Nancyne

It Only Took A Hyperthyroid, Malaria, and Near Death To Wake Me Up…
Susan Jacobs

A confluence of early influences and events led me to a lifetime of seeking the truth, my truth. Perhaps it was two near death experiences, or exposure to yoga, Transcendental Meditation, and astrology circa the 1970s when I was young, or maybe it was experiencing different cultures while travelling in Europe, Africa, and Haiti.

The irony; I was a liar?

I loved lying and spun a great yarn. As a closet writer, it was creating the complex and elaborate backstory around each lie that gave me a rush. The lies were intricate; keeping track of them almost required a spreadsheet. The irony with lying is that you really start to believe that your lie is the truth, even though you know it's not.

Most lies were around things I wasn't proud of… like bailing on a friend's birthday party, or not telling the truth about some guy I was messing around with, stuff like that.

The more damaging lies though, were the ones I convinced myself were true about me.

I spent decades attempting to 'fit in' and be 'normal,' yet felt like an outside observer of my life rather than an active, decision-making participant. Some examples… Marriage was not on my 'to do' list, yet I got married in my mid-20s, divorced by 30, and remarried three years later. I worked as a temp word processor and serendipitously landed a great career in the entertainment industry doing marketing and publicity, but never stopped to think about what I really wanted to do with my life.

I had fantasies about being an investigative reporter or living on an ashram in India as a yogi but was too chicken to take that decisive stand. I got involved with emotionally and verbally abusive men and allowed it, because I thought that's what I deserved.

In 2004, when I first met Krishna Kaur, my Kundalini yoga teacher, she said, 'You're a dancer.' Excited that it was obvious, I enthusiastically said, 'Yes! I do African dance, I love the drums and blah, blah, blah.' She stopped me dead in my tracks and said, 'No, you've been dancing around yourself to avoid facing your truth for years.'

She saw right through me after just a few hours of knowing each other, and was absolutely right.

I'd always been a free spirit – going where life took me, telling myself, 'things happen for a reason,' and hoping to find myself along the way.

Over the years, I came to realize that we are the architects of our lives so it's best to build on a foundation of truth, not lies.

I didn't want to commit to anything for fear I'd miss out on something else, something better, or find out that I wasn't good enough. I was passionate about so much but non-committal, so I flip-flopped around.

Despite outward appearances, for years, I wrestled with self-doubt, insecurity, fear, and lack of self-love. I didn't listen to my gut, allowed myself to be treated disrespectfully, and was often frustrated, feeling like I was having an out-of-life experience, imagining there must be more but not knowing what or how to access it.

Despite how I perceived myself, friends and people I met along the way said I'm a force to reckon with, others were inspired by my life, and a few thought I was crazy. Perception is a funny thing; how others see us is rarely how we see ourselves.

Deadly Insect Bite #1…

When I opened my eyes, half-a-dozen doctors stood over me taking turns anxiously saying, "You just died. You're allergic to xylocaine. You went into anaphylactic shock, your heart stopped."

Huh? I didn't know what had happened but this was not the best way to welcome someone back to life. Were they trying to kill me a second time?

A strange bug bite prompted me to have it checked out at a hospital in Jacksonville, Florida during a family vacation when I was 15. The doctor said he would numb my foot to remove a stinger. Next thing I knew, my lights were out and no one was home. They resuscitated me with adrenaline that kept me buzzing for days but still made me spend the night for observations. I was released the next day and our vacation resumed.

When back home, it was fun to tell friends that I had died during Easter break.

My first near death experience didn't sink in for years – it was just a cool story I shared. But something inside me knew it meant more; I was here for a reason.

Your Body Don't Lie…

Pop star Shakira sings, "My hips don't lie." For me, it was my thyroid, a tiny, yet hugely important gland that regulates our endocrine system.

I swallowed my truth over and over and over again until my thyroid had enough; it had to get my attention, and it did. I developed a raging hyperthyroid (throat) and Graves' disease (eyes). It was now the second time I potentially faced my mortality. My whole system was on overdrive, with my resting heartbeat over 100 BPM.

Standard treatment is to drink radioactive iodine to kill the thyroid and then you become hypothyroid and need medicine for life. No, thank you.

I was certain that I could heal myself holistically and believed that I developed these conditions for a reason. I was determined to figure out how and why.

With this serious health condition, it was the first time that I stood up for my life and didn't care what anyone thought.

It was an extremely difficult journey but a force within me emerged. Although at times I questioned if I was making the right decision, I never changed course.

I fully stood in my conviction that I could heal myself, despite what doctors, family, and friends believed true.

My endocrinologist said I was risking my life and fired me as a patient for being reckless, but I ultimately proved him wrong.

I knew I developed a hyperthyroid and Graves' disease for a reason. What ultimately transformed my healing and started to balance my thyroid after years of working with countless alternative/holistic healers and experimenting with various spiritual paths was the result of a single book.

An Ah-Ha moment came when reading about the Fifth Chakra, located in the throat, in Carolyn Myss's book "Anatomy of the Spirit." I asked myself, "Why did I get conditions that attacked my throat and eyes? What am I not saying and seeing in my life?"

In that moment, I realized how lost and unhappy I was and that my lies, or rather avoiding my truth, were metaphorically strangling me. The thing with having those kinds of life-altering realizations is that once you're aware, you can no longer hide. In yoga, they say happiness is a birthright, not a myth; I wanted true happiness and the inner peace that it brings.

It was time to take stock, clean house, and make drastic changes, which included quitting my job, leaving my second husband, going to Ghana, West Africa for two months, breaking up with some friends, deleting people from my address book, a lot of meditating, yoga, soul-searching, and writing.

Most importantly, I stopped lying and started to own, speak, and live my truth. It became accessible when I got really honest with myself. Clarity, integrity, and I got very intimate. I could finally articulate what I wanted, what mattered to me, the types of people that lite me up, and the kind of person I wanted to be.

It was an existential roller-coaster ride, a long, challenging, eye-opening, and empowering journey. But on the other side, my thyroid remains intact and balanced, and I'm medication-free. On most days, internal peace and happiness are my natural state of mind.

Deadly Insect Bite #2…

In 2005, I had a second near-death experience from severe malaria in Ghana where I was doing my Kundalini yoga teacher training program with Krishna Kaur. A single mosquito from the universe of mosquitos flattened me.

Minutes from dead, an African Ayurveda doctor saved my life through an herbal treatment protocol. I would have likely died if taken to the hospital instead of his clinic because of the slow-moving intake process.

Years later, reading an old journal, I found an entry from 10 days before the trip describing a dream where I got malaria. Did I will this and manifest that one mosquito? Getting sick in Africa was a huge fear, especially after reading the CDC travel warnings. Malaria has a 10-day incubation period; I got hit on day 10 so must have been bitten upon arrival.

This gave me pause, reinforcing my belief that we are active participants in creating our reality, and our thoughts do have power.

This life-changing experience allowed me to face and overcome my fear, and thankfully, it had a happy ending. The doctor was incredibly knowledgeable and literally had my life in his hands. He treated me like family and remains a dear friend.

I wondered though what it meant that insect bites were involved both times I almost died. Certain it wasn't just coincidence, I had to dig deeper within for answers.

The Early Years…

Why was it so hard to trust and believe in myself, to own, speak, and live my truth. What was I afraid of?

My family was unusual. My parents didn't have conventional day jobs. Dad was an award-winning photographer, made two films (one is in the Museum of Modern Art's permanent collection), and then co-founded with my mom, who was a painter, the Earth Shoe company – the 'shoe of the hippies' in the '70s.

My sister and I went to the United Nations International School from elementary through high school so our friends were from around the globe, and the kids of UN diplomats. By 17, I'd been to Europe four times; on three family vacations and the fourth trip was my high school graduation present.

My home life was grounded in love, encouragement, fun, and possibility but underscored with the ups and downs of the creative, artistic, entrepreneurial life that I experienced through my parents. It's what I knew, was drawn to, and terrified of.

For as long as I can remember, I've been a writer, albeit a closet one. It's in my DNA. I was trying to find my voice and point of view through writing but didn't have the confidence to share it. So I swallowed that truth about myself.

Afraid to commit to being a writer, I had no idea what else to do with my life, or how to think of myself. There was never that certainty of what I was going to do when I grew up. Even in mid-life, sometimes I still wonder!

My parents encouraged my sister and I to explore our creativity; they never pressured us about careers, marriage, and kids. We were given a lot of freedom, maybe too much, and very little discipline. I took full advantage.

After college, I was directionless; I turned to sex, drugs, and rock 'n roll, got a tattoo, a dog, my first apartment, sold sunglasses on the street, and became a roller disco queen. I always had lots going on but felt empty inside; something was missing… Me!

Spiritual teachers and holistic healers started turning up. Alternative treatments combined with martial arts, spirituality, connecting more with my own internal wisdom, and tuning into the mind/body relationship, started to ground me and bring clarity. I was looking for answers, direction, and purpose.

Always a work-in-progress, the path through the hyperthyroid and Graves' helped me figure out who I really am. It also helped me discover what I want to accomplish in this lifetime, my purpose, my why, and the legacy I want to leave behind. Although it sucked at times, I held onto believing that there was a hidden treasure in the journey, that if I could access it, my life would be forever changed.

Here a few reminders that helped me along the way. Perhaps you'll find them useful on your path to uncover, embrace, and fully live your truth too.

Be willing to get uncomfortable

Let go of expectations and judgment

Vulnerability takes courage and the rewards are worth it

Feelings aren't facts

Meditation works. Journaling works.

Be unapologetic in your quest to find, speak, and live your truth

Always remember that your voice, and being matters.

So really, as writer Ray Bradbury said, "What's there to lose in jumping and developing your wings on the way down?"

About the Author

Giving voice to things that matter, raising awareness, and expanding perspectives is the heart and soul of who Susan is and what she does. She believes everybody has a story that deserves to be heard.

As someone who swallowed her truth for decades and ultimately developed a hyperthyroid and Graves' disease where her thyroid metaphorically strangled her, Susan was forced to face her own truth and find her voice. She healed herself holistically during a long journey where she learned to navigate and integrate Western and Eastern medicine for her own healing.

Susan is a writer, storyteller, strategist, and producer with more than 25 years of marketing, branding, communications, writing, and business experience. She has traveled the world seeking adventures and worked on projects in Haiti, Africa, Europe, and across the U.S. Her years of expertise are enriched by the life-changing experiences she has had in different cultures while traveling off the beaten path.

Throughout her career, Susan has been a writer both professionally and personally. She is a contributing author to the book, 'Pain, Purpose, Passion; That Was Then, This is Now' and has a book publishing deal with The Round House Press for which she is working on her first memoir. Her writing has been published in FourTwoNine magazine, IndieWire, Aquarian Times magazine, Spirituality & Health magazine, and PR Week. She is a contributing blogger to Huffington Post and Thrive Global, and a guest blogger for Identity magazine and Yogic Living. Susan is a salsa dancer and holds certifications in Kundalini yoga, Pilates, and as a Shiatsu massage therapist. She lives by this quote from Yogi Bhajan, "You should make yourself so happy that by looking at you other people become happy."

Email Address: susan@bluezanconsulting.com

Phone Number: 1-917-626-5999

http://www.givingvoicetothingsthatmatter.com

www.bluezanconsulting.com

LinkedIn Page: www.linkedin.com/in/susanjacobs7

Twitter handle: www.twitter.com/susanjwrites

If You Believe...The Magical Marketer
Julia Stege, MFA

I don't know what took me so long. Ever since I was a young child I had fantasies of singing and acting in musicals, and I'd stuck my toe in the water a couple times. But I always had that negative self-talk, "You don't know what you're doing. You're not as good a singer as those other kids." And just to confirm this, my mother who was quite a good singer in her own right, used to tell me I was singing flat. This stopped me for a long, long, very long time.

I had other creative pursuits and I followed those diligently. Yet, I ignored my diva calling, except in the shower when I usually belt one out for the shampoo bottles and soap dish... or walking home alone from school, I would start singing and twirling occasionally as I walked, like Julie Andrews on the mountain top with the cameraman flying overhead.

Don't get me wrong, I have a very creative career as a designer, writer and marketing consultant. I get to work with people in whatever way I'm called to do. I don't have to follow what any boss tells me (which used to get me into trouble back in the day when I had bosses!) But that Barbra Streisand part of me was just gathering dust on the shelf.

Then I got 'older and older and older.' About 40 years older and I noticed I wasn't doing fun things that are just about fun, that didn't have anything to do with work. I always have had a passion for my business, but when I was trying to think what else I was energized about in life, I asked my husband and he said, 'work.' and I said, **"What else?"** And he said, **"Work."**

The more I worked, the more isolated I became. Till I was wrapped in my head, all tight like a nut and frequently I woke up in the middle of

the night consumed with worry. (This is what happens when we repress our full creative selves, I discovered.)

Luckily, I got some help, I joined a local women's mastermind and got the support I needed to explore my passion. I mean, I love my work, which is great but that's not all there is to life!

Fast forward a year and a half and there I am standing in the spotlight of a small local theater production of The Wiz, playing Glinda the Good Witch, donned in golden sequins and a sparkling train, a lighted crown and holding a 6-foot-tall glittering staff.

Let me say as a caveat that my usual outfit is more like pajamas. But I took to this glittering array like a born diva, a goddess in my own right.

The spotlight is bright and this makes me a little dizzy, in a good way. I lift up my eyes and grab hold of the microphone.

And I'm singing. "Believe you can go home. Believe you can float on air. Just click your heels three times, if you believe, then you'll be there." It's as if the song were written for me, it's so totally aligned with my soul. In the play I am uplifting Dorothy, the Lion, Scarecrow and 'Tin-woman.' They thought they needed the Wiz to fix them, to give them home, some courage, a brain and a heart. **All they need is to believe in themselves.**

My voice is echoing throughout the theater and I see the grinning faces of friends and strangers alike and I feel like I AM floating on air. A kind of happiness is welling inside of me greater than I remember experiencing before.

As the band plays louder, my backup singers come out holding glittering stars, and they're singing with me, "Believe in yourself right from the start. Believe in the magic that's inside your heart. Believe all these things not because we told you to, but believe in yourself…"

I look up and the whole theater is alive and believing and smiling and I'm basking in the light and expressing myself at the highest level possible, "As I believe in you."

I had been practicing this song for four months, every day, several times, a day. It became like a mantra for me, uplifting me and carrying me forward to the moment when I'd reveal this part of myself to the world, my diva debut.

And when that moment came, it felt perfect. I was magical, my tone was good and the message was clear. When I swung up an octave to hit that last note, I was glowing and the whole room exploded in cheers. I was being my goddess self and I was shining!

And was it perfect? I mean, would I have wanted Simon Cowell there judging me? No way. But this is what I discovered; I don't have to be technically perfect as a singer and actor to move my audience.

People came streaming up to me afterward to thank me. One woman from the senior center came by in her wheelchair and grabbed my hand and held it wordless, smiling, and nodding.

So, when I got the video from the producer, I couldn't wait to watch it. But when I did, that old critic came up again, my old 'friend,' and I was cringing. And crying, because the memory of it is so touching to me, and the song is such a reminder of what I'm all about, really. And I was thinking, I can't show this video to anyone. It's not perfect enough. Maybe I'll just enjoy it myself.

Do you ever do that… create something that is such a self-expression that it brings tears to your eyes; then instead of sending it out to share with the world, you hold it close to your chest and don't show anyone?

This is the problem I think we all face at some point or another, a fear around really showing up going for it even when we're not perfect. So we keep trying and trying and trying to perfect our expression, holding it close to our heart but never showing anyone. And when we do that years can go by and we haven't gotten to share that part of ourselves with people.

I made this mistake in my business, too. **For many years I hid my 'woo' self for fear certain clients would think I was crazy.** And this was a key reason that I hit my own 5-figure glass ceiling for so long. My Soul Tribe couldn't find me…or if they did find me they couldn't recognize me because I was hiding out and not being fully ME.

I had to realize a few things and ultimately "come out" as me through my marketing before I started attracting my tribe and finally broke through my own financial glass ceiling. I had to realize that if 'like attracts like' my perfect customers are like me. Therefore, I had to let go of the idea that everyone must relate to me, including lawyers and dentists. I decided that if I can attract anyone (and I can), I choose to attract highly creative magical visionaries who have new ways to transform people's lives and the world.

Most importantly, I realized I must be authentic for my tribe to even recognize me! To start a conversation with my Soul Tribe, I had to reveal my own Soul in the process. A very vulnerable activity indeed. Once I did this, and truly came out as me, I began attracting people who are in alignment with my purpose. Because we are aligned, I am uniquely qualified to create their Wildly Attractive Brand & Website ... one that reflects their authenticity and forwards their soul's purpose in the world.

I speak with hundreds of spiritually business women and conscious entrepreneurs who are hiding out like this, so afraid to authentically put themselves out there. It makes sense when you've been misunderstood your whole life. It takes a brave soul who is committed to making a difference to actually step forward and shine online, and that is what is needed in this crazy world we live in. **Our soul's work will change the world, if we let it; b**ut how to overcome the fear and just do it? Here are some steps that have helped me and thousands of other heart-based entrepreneurs around the world come through the fear and SHINE!

1. **Discover your Soul Tribe.** When you discover who you were born to serve, who you are uniquely qualified to help, it clears your plate of everyone who simply doesn't get you or is not interested in you at all.

2. **I found that sharing my magical self and my diva self was much easier when I let go of needing everyone to like me and focusing instead on those I am aligned with, who want to hear my message, my voice.**

3. **Identify Your Essence, What Makes You Tick.** When you identify what is most inspiring to you, what is most important in your life, what your Soul is desiring, and you share that with others, you will naturally draw in those who are aligned with your message. And when you focus on your passion and purpose, letting go things that are less important to you, you are free to be yourself, express yourself, without worry of how others will respond.

4. **Clarify What You Really Want.** It's a revolutionary question for most women to ask, "What's perfect for me?" Simply because we have been trained to be concerned about other people's needs, often before our own. We grow up so 'other focused' that we do not have the time or space to consider our own needs and desires. I'm asking you to do this now so that you can begin focusing in the positive direction of your dreams. The more your actions are in alignment with your dreams, the happier you will be on the journey, and the less you will hold back from stepping forward to shine.

By the way, I did share that video of me as Glinda after all. I decided it was a matter of integrity that I shouldn't hold back when I'm asking others to not hold back. And the response was so beautiful, I was moved to tears. I would have never known how much my community supports my self-expression if I hadn't shared it.

What are you holding back from the world? I urge you to share it, even if it scares you. If one person is moved, it makes the whole thing worthwhile. I promise you. You'll love it in the light.

If you would like more support on your journey, there is a magical toolkit I would like to share with you that can help you with the steps I've shared above. You can get it at http://www.magicalmarketingtoolkit.com

About the Author

Julia Stege helps **out-of-the-box entrepreneurs and change-makers** to clarify and express **their purpose** through marketing that attracts their perfect customers from across the globe. Her magical realm of talent is branding and creating inspired websites for clients who are as serious about attracting divinely aligned clients online as they are about changing the world. **Since 1997, hundreds of clients** united in their desire to show up authentically in their marketing have worked with Julia to showcase what makes them special and distinct online. Their Wildly Attractive Websites™ serve as magnets that attract leads, clients, and difference-making opportunities from around the world.

Email Address: julia@magical-marketing.com

Website Address: www.magical-marketing.com

Phone Number: (510) 30-MAGIC

Website Facebook page(s): https://www.facebook.com/MagicalMarketer/

LinkedIn Page https://www.linkedin.com/in/magicalmarketer/

Twitter handle @magicalmarketer

YouTube Channel http://www.youtube.com/c/JuliaStegeMagic

Other Contact Information Channels

Pinterest: https://www.pinterest.com/magicalmarketer/boards/

Instagram: https://www.instagram.com/juliastege/

Step Into Your Passion!
Laurie Ratto, RN, HTCP, CCA

Have you ever asked yourself the question: "Why am I doing this?" Or felt like what you are doing no longer feeds your soul even though it did so in the past? If yes, then this chapter is for you. I have discovered that **if you feel something in your life is no longer fulfilling, you can explore the things you're drawn too and create the life that truly aligns with you and your passions.** Can I share my story of how I discovered this? After working as an RN in conventional medicine for over 30 years I chose to become a holistic practitioner with my own private healing practice! Now I am an integrative medicine specialist and teach health care professionals and caregivers holistic therapies plus work with clients. Several things transpired over the course of 3 years that lead me to change and I have never looked back. I am honored to share my story with you, including the challenges in hopes you will not have the same issues. I have discovered, **once you find something that fills your soul and you're passionate about don't let anyone tell you not to do it.**

I had been working in hospitals and home health for about 29 years and loved what I did. Yes, there were crazy days when I came home exhausted but overall what I received back emotionally, mentally and financially from patients, co-workers and the facility made me feel great inside.

When I was around 48 I injured by neck, upper back and shoulder which resulted in chronic pain. I chose not to take prescription or over the counter medications on a regular basis because I had seen the damage they could do long term. I chose to immerse myself in learning about holistic therapies to help alleviate/manage my pain. I had been interested in complementary medicine since I was 20 but didn't pursue it at that time because I knew people and facilities were not very accepting of it then.

Around this same time, I started to feel less fulfilled at work. I was working as an RN in the Emergency room which could be very chaotic. Over the years my time at the bedside became less and the connection I made with my patients frequently did not nourish my soul. I missed the deeper connection with people, learning about them and helping them to feel better in a variety of ways. I no longer thrived in chaos and felt like I was sticking people with needles, pushing pills and running out of the room to the next person. **This was not what I wanted to be doing or who I wanted to be.** As time went on I found myself starting to judge some patients and being less empathetic. **I knew something needed to change**.

Searching for ways to alleviate my physical pain I came across a 2-day Healing Touch class which is an energy medicine therapy. At the end of the 2nd day I knew that was to be my next path in life, helping people to heal holistically! **This therapy allowed me to connect deeply with others, alleviate all forms of pain in a <u>gentle, non-invasive</u> manner and it would be easier on my physical body.** I started working with a healing touch practitioner to alleviate my own pain. **Using this therapy combined with aromatherapy I was able to resolve my chronic pain and knew I wanted to help others do the same.**

I continued to take healing touch classes and started practicing on friends and family and getting positive results. Once I felt more confident doing the work I started working on nursing colleagues. One evening I was working on a nurse at work because she was having rib pain. It was her first evening back to work after being thrown from her horse resulting in bruised ribs. As I worked on her I could feel the MD watching me. When I turned to work on the nurse's other side and made eye contact with the MD he said, "What voodoo are you doing?" **The nurse turned in her chair and said, "It's healing touch, it is making my pain go away so be quiet and let her finish!" I just smiled.**

Once I became a certified practitioner I used healing touch on patients in the ER. I was able to help patients decrease anxiety, pain and muscle tension. In the beginning the doctors were very skeptical and sometimes annoyed with me for doing the work. However, when they saw the blood pressure, heart rate and breathing rate decrease as I worked and witnessed the positive results for the patient they started to ask me to work on certain patients. **I helped patients take the edge off of their pain when there was going to be a time lag before the doctor could see them or until the pill they received could kick in. Others were very anxious; I helped to calm them without medications.**

All of this took me **out of my comfort zone**. I was performing a service that most were unfamiliar with and that MDs didn't approve of. **I had to believe in myself, the therapies and the innate healing ability of the body.** At the time we did not have a lot of research about healing touch and we still cannot measure the subtle energy field so several staff members did not support or believe in what I did. **I knew that it was effective, safe and could help patients so I continued to do the work.** Then the universe actually pushed me out of the ER into my healing practice.

I developed frozen shoulder in my right arm so I could not work. I could only raise my arm about 40 degrees. The orthopedic MD said if he did surgery I could be back to work in less than a month or I could let it heal naturally which would take about a year. I opted for the natural approach.

During this time off I formally started studying aromatherapy (essential oils) to become a certified clinical aroma-therapist. I had been using essential oils on myself and family members for 2 years with good results and wanted to offer that to clients as well.

Recovery from the frozen shoulder was much faster than anticipated. I receiving physical therapy and used aromatherapy, healing touch and guided imagery to resolve my issue 90% in 6 months! However, as my right shoulder was healing my left shoulder started to freeze up. My left shoulder took 7 months to resolve 90%. **After being off work for just over 1 year I realized I could not return to that chaotic environment. I had not understood how it had been affecting me emotionally, mentally and spiritually until I was out of it for a period of time. It was suffocating me and my spirit, plus it was hard on my physical body.** Turning and lifting patients that couldn't help themselves caused me to come home some nights with painful back or shoulders. I would be emotionally exhausted some nights or feel hardened other nights. Don't get me wrong, I still had some very gratifying times but those were occurring less and less and the administration wanted us to do more and more. So the vast difference I felt in my physical and emotional being after being off work for a year told me not to return. My friends working there told me not to return, that things had gotten even worse.

That is when I spoke with my husband about quitting and opening my own practice. We agreed on a time frame of 3 years to get my business up and running. After that I would have to get a part time job if my practice was not bringing in money.

I knew the work I did would benefit many and that many people were looking for alternatives to medications. What I did not know was how to set-up a practice, market myself and charge for services. **As an RN in a hospital or home health agency patients were abundant and came to us. Now I had to find a way to let people know my business existed and to pay me.**

This was totally foreign to me. I had thought everyone would just flock to me because who wants to be in pain but I was wrong. People were not educated about these therapies and they didn't know my business existed. Before the hospital or agency paid me, not an individual and doesn't everyone deserve to be healthy? *How can I charge for something I think everyone should have access to and that insurance does not pay for? How was I going to make a living if I did not charge enough? As an RN I made a decent living.* **One of my biggest struggles was pricing my services.** I discovered I didn't have to figure this out on my own.

I enrolled in a program that helped me to learn how to market my business, speak publically to educate and obtain clients and determine my fee. **This foundation allowed me to start my business.** I am grateful for that experience. I made many friends and started to feel more empowered, able to speak my truth about health and healing, confident in myself and my work.

I was scared and determined to make this work. I started speaking to many different groups to educate people and promote my services. I went to networking groups. **I was not comfortable doing any of this when I started but by remembering what I wanted to accomplish and how it could help people I pushed myself to do it. Sometimes we have to do things that are uncomfortable in order for us to grow.**

In the beginning I worked with people 1:1 to alleviate physical or emotional pain. The majority of my clients were able to decrease or eliminate the amount of medication they took while being more active. Others who had come in feeling "stuck" or depressed were able to move forward in their life and feel more upbeat. There were some that did not experience a significant change in their pain. That was the hardest for me personally. Had I done something wrong? Did I miss something? Was I as good a practitioner/healer as I was a nurse? Should I continue to do this work?

Having the support of other healers really helped me at this point. My mentor, teachers and other practitioners in the area were a sounding board for me to ask questions, talk about situations that arose, express my fears and celebrate my successes. Without this type of support, I don't know if I would have continued on. **Doing something that is not mainstream or widely accepted can cause you to doubt yourself and your mission.**

Being around supportive and like-minded people helped me to stay focused and committed.

To help me continue my personal and business growth I discovered a coaching and mastermind group that really resonated with me. **We worked on our inner game, business, money, self-worth and more. This was a powerful combination which helped me to stand in my power and claim myself as an expert.** I realized I really wanted to be working with health care professionals and caregivers. I wanted to teach them the therapies so even more people could be healed and they could take better care of themselves too.

I became an instructor of Healing Touch and aromatherapy. This allowed me to teach about self-care for care givers (my stealth mission) by giving them concrete things they can do for themselves so that they can keep helping others. A few students have even chosen to work with me one on one, to improve their physical or emotional health. I feel blessed to be able to do this work.

The truths I want to pass on to you are:

1. Never be afraid to do what you are passionate about.
2. Find others with the same passion and support one another.
3. Get help in any area you feel is needed.
4. Don't wait for others to approve of what you are doing.

Stepping forward may not be the easiest or most comfortable thing you ever do but it will be a journey well worth it. Be still, listen to your heart, discover your passion and take steps to incorporate it into your life.

About the Author

Laurie Ratto is a change agent for health care. An RN for over 35 years, she resolved her own chronic pain and stress with integrative medicine (holistic therapies plus conventional medicine). What she learned made such a profound difference in her life she decided she must share it with others and became a holistic practitioner. She has been a holistic practitioner for over a decade and has helped thousands of people. She understands the importance of addressing the mind, body and spirit for healing. Her passion is two-fold: Assisting individuals to reduce physical, mental and emotional pain using a toolbox of holistic therapies. The other is to bring integrative medicine into all types of health care facilities by teaching health professionals, caregivers and lay people holistic therapies.

She has worked with clients one-on-one across the US and in Europe. She has taught classes at many facilities including UCSF, Mission Hospice, and the Osher Center for Integrative Medicine and Kaiser.

She wants everyone to achieve their highest level of wellness. She teaches people skills they can use the rest of their life to help decrease stress, improve health and well-being. Laurie says, "I see all of you – not just your physical body. When you see all of you, you will feel empowered to manage your health and wellness and help others do the same."

She is a certified clinical aroma-therapist, healing touch certified practitioner/instructor and certified in guided imagery. When she is not working with clients 1:1, speaking or teaching classes she loves spending time with her family, being out in nature and playing with their dog Huck.

laurie@mindandbodymethod.com

510 381-3191

www.mindandbodymethod.com

www.facebook.com/mindandbodymethod/

www.linkedin.com/in/laurie-ratto-rn

Change Your Story; Change Your Life
LeaAnn Fuller

I was once told that I was one of the hardest and most talented coaches in the industry. However, my bank account wasn't showing it. I was making a difference but not getting paid for it. Other than making money I was really on top of the world and making a difference through speaking, as a #1 International Best-Selling Author, a Coach, and I even had my own radio show. But you wouldn't know it if you had taken a look at my bank account.

I was finally beginning to come out of the shadows that I had been hiding in and letting my true light shine. I really thought that I had overcome all of the fears that had kept me hidden for years from the spotlight. Or so I thought but something deep down subconsciously was keeping me hidden from the life that I desired.

It has taken the time to dig deep and realize that I was struggling with some serious inner issues that paralyze so many of us. Many of us keep ourselves hidden in the shadows for these inner issues. We all have them, they just look different for each of us. One thing for sure though is that if we aren't living the life we desire it is our fear that paralyzes us, even if we don't know it. If we are stuck, we need to really sit with ourselves and ask what it is that we are resisting? What resistance has us paralyzed to what it is that we truly can be?

What is holding us back from being the powerful women that we are destined to be? As, we are all destined for greatness. We wouldn't be given this vision of a higher purpose if we weren't meant to live it. So, what is stopping us? So, what was stopping me? What was keeping me stuck? What was I resisting? My answers were so full of I don't knows.

I have learned a lot along this journey to self-discovery. One of the biggest lessons that I learned was that if our answers are constantly "I don't know", as mine seemed to be, then we're not being true to ourselves. "I don't know" are just words that we use to build walls, so we can protect ourselves from the scary truths that we are holding deep within to keep us safe. We think these walls or words are protecting us but in fact we are doing ourselves a tremendous injustice because all we are doing is holding back and denying ourselves deep inner discovery and growth. We are denying ourselves the truth that we need to really move on and live our dreams.

The walls that we put up to protect us from what has been hidden deep down has served us in the past. For that we can be grateful because it has gotten us where we are now. To elevate ourselves to the next level of our lives we need to tear down the walls that hold us back. We need to tear them down brick by brick and discover what every brick and every I don't know was built with and why. **We need to breakthrough every 'I don't know' one at a time with courage and genuine curiosity. Let our 'I don't knows' become our tools to discovery and perseverance.**

Discovering the "I don't knows", the hidden, the subconscious tendencies is a scary but empowering journey. If they weren't scary then we wouldn't have built the walls around them. But a journey like no other if we become vulnerable enough to truly endure and embrace them, peeling them back one layer at a time. They will give us the insight that we need to move ahead and conquer the demons and fears that are holding us back.

I say endure because it is tough work. Seeking the truth about our 'I don't knows' is as mentally challenging as it would be physically challenging tearing down an actual wall. Once you begin to scratch the surface of these I don't knows you can figure out what is keeping you from discovering what truths are hidden there and why you are hiding from them.

I know for me it was one of the most overwhelming experiences that I have ever experienced, and I was overcome with tears when I finally started to recognize what was really going on. It literally took my breath away as I fought off my fight or flight instinct.

This is where it is so important to really sit in our own vulnerability because it is so easy to stop dead and skip back to the I don't know as we are fighting back the tears and tightening in our chest with the nearly unbearable OMG feeling. It's like getting hit with an avalanche of voices in our heads, fears, feelings, and emotions that we have been holding back for years.

This is where we can and will uncover the fears and self-doubt that is holding us captive in the shadows. Our deepest fears of failure or even success. We can so easily get caught up with what others will think of us when we put ourselves out there. Like who the do we think we are? We are definitely nothing special. Or even them realizing that we are not perfect. What would happen if they uncovered the skeletons in our closet? Because let's face it, no one is perfect and we all have made mistakes but that is what makes us who we are and that is what qualifies us to step forward and shine. After all, we can never promise to be perfect, we can only promise to be real.

While we are digging into the "I don't knows" we need to pay attention to who's voices we hear when we are telling ourselves that we can't do it or that we aren't good enough. We all have them but don't even realize it. They are living deep below the "I don't knows" within our subconscious. They are the voices we hear within our inner dialog that is keeping us from being great. **It is important to discover what may be behind these 'I don't knows' so that we can change the conversation.** We can take this opportunity to show the evidence from everything that we have overcome and how far we have already made it to prove to those in our head telling us otherwise that they are wrong. WE can tell them and show them that WE CAN DO IT no matter what they say. **We can show that we are strong, amazing, and most of all we deserve to really live the life that we desire.**

If we are afraid of someone asking us, who do we think we are or telling us, we are not good enough, whose voice is it that we are hearing? Who we are hearing is most likely someone from our childhood. It is so important we recognize and acknowledge who and what it is so that we can begin to work on it, where it is coming from and why.

We subconsciously harbor what we saw and heard from our childhood and it can affect everything that we do now. Our parent's words and actions, even unintentionally, sculpted us into the women that we are today. If we grew up in a family of poverty and watching our family struggle at everything, that is what we know. It is what our subconscious knows and no matter what we think we want that is what our subconscious is comfortable. Let's face it different can be scary so unless we are brave enough to face it the struggle that our subconscious is comfortable with is what we will live.

For me it was watching my mom struggle working two and three jobs at a time to make ends meet and raise us after my dad passed. It was a challenge to realize that after watching her work eighty plus hours a week and barely sleeping to just barely get by turned into struggle for me. It was a challenge to realize that I had that, just barely getting by, mindset in my life. This translated to me that nothing comes easy, it isn't supposed to be easy. Life is supposed to be hard.

The voice inside my head is my mom telling me, be safe, realistic, work hard, and you will get by one way or another. You are a survivor.

It has taken me time to retrain my mind and my subconscious to know that I can do more than survive, I can thrive. There is so much more out there in life for me than struggle and I am not meant to live my life in poverty and struggle. I had to train my mind to change the conversation in my head that I hear when I hear my mom.

Now the dialog in my head with my mom is her telling me that she didn't work so hard and struggle to watch me work that hard and struggle. She worked hard so that I hopefully wouldn't have to and could have the better life that I deserve. If anyone deserves it that I do. She is proud of me. I have the power and the strength to make a difference in lives of others that no one else can. I am meant to make a difference in this world. **Be great and Be powerful. If anyone can do it, it is you. Come out of the shadows to step forward and shine.**

Here are the key steps to retrain your brain and SHINE:

- Check to see if you are hiding?
- If yes, explore what you are hiding from; afraid of?
- If you discover some "I don't knows" recognize this is another way to hide, and be willing to explore what is underneath.
- Get support if you feel stuck and aren't able to see what may be holding you back.

Recognize and celebrate when you discover what is holding you back and be willing to release it. (Sometime we hold on to old stories and ways of being that no longer serve.)

Be willing to release what no longer serves and embrace what does serve.

Step forward and THIRVE!

About the Author

LeaAnn Fuller is a Women's Transformational and Fuller Life Coach, Amazon #1 International Best-Selling Author, Motivational Speaker, and Radio Show Host. She is the founder of Fuller Life, LLC where she travels empowering women to get out of their own way to transform their life, find their greatness, and to live their Fuller Life. She empowers them to find clarity about what it is they want, why they want it, and what is standing in their way so that they can quit living small and begin living their Fuller Life.

LeaAnn is a graduate of Coach U's Core Essential Program for Personal and Corporate Coach Training. She has an extensive background in business management, new business set-up, accounting, and sales.

LeaAnn is a #1 International Best-Selling Co-Author of The Unstoppable Woman of Purpose, DIVAS, and many more. She is a weekly radio show host of Welcome to Your Fuller Life on Sage Network.

LeaAnn is also the founder of Adopt-A-Mom for Christmas, in memory of her mother, that has been able to give back to hundreds of moms in need over the holidays. She in planning on turning this program into a year-round movement to support single and struggling moms year-round. She is also the Program Director for WBOC, The Premier Organization for Women in Business in CNY.

Email Address: leaann@welcometoyourfullerlife.com

Phone Number: 315-825-5859

Website: https://lovingyourfullerlife.com/

Facebook page(s): https://www.facebook.com/FullerLifeLLC/

Linked in: https://www.linkedin.com/in/leaann-fuller-9a42b8a0/

Twitter https://twitter.com/FullerLifeCoach

Radio show: www.blogtalkradio.com/sagenetwork

The Rise Of The Feminine: 'SHE' Power
Jennevieve Ybarra, MA

In a room full of a hundred women, the facilitator asked the question: "How many of you grew up knowing that your sexuality is a safe sacred place?" Please raise your hand. The room fell so silent you could hear a pin drop. As I looked around the room, I was in awe to see that only two women had raised their hand. Shivers ran up my spine and a silent tear fell from my eye.

The sadness I felt at the time reminded me, not only myself but of a client of mine, a woman sixty-one years of age who before we started working together, had never known love. My heart broke upon learning this. For reasons such as the aforementioned, I created *Feminine Mojo, Find Your 'SHE' Spot.*

'SHE' Spot is

S- **S**overeignty, **S**exual healing and empowerment

H- **H**appiness

E- **E**xtraordinary love & romantic relationships

Feminine Mojo is the first thing that people see when they meet you. It is your relentless confidence, radiance and vitality. It is about living your life through deep rooted Feminine Principles to live in your truth, your wisdom, and feminine power.

Feminine Mojo, Find Your 'SHE' Spot is about living your life designed by your desires, bringing the Divine Feminine to all your relationships and stepping into even more of your greatness to have the prosperous life, love, and deep connection and intimacy you desire.

Have you heard of the Triple Goddess archetype the Maiden, Mother and Crone? Each represents the stages in a woman's life. Part of knowing and participating in our Feminine Power is being able to access any of these at will. I use these as well as other feminine archetypes in my coaching practice. Working with archetypes is powerful work because being able to embody the different aspects of ourselves is key to wholeness and sovereignty. We have many roles that we play and it is important to not only access them but to join them as well. If you shrink in one area of your life, you shrink in all areas of your life because wherever you are, there you are.

Recently I had the pleasure of having my mother in one of my workshops titled, *Embrace Your Venus, Goddess of Love, Beauty & Sexuality*. She represented the Crone who is the older, silver-haired wise one whose deep wisdom has been cultivated over a lifetime. During her share, her words broke my heart and at the same time inspired me. As she began to speak, no words came out but rather tears. Through her tears she said, "I am seventy years old and I am crying because I am just now learning about this [opening to our voice of truth and sexuality]." She went on, "because in my era we were taught to," and she gestured, putting her hand over her mouth, "to keep quiet." The reason I felt my heart break was because as her daughter, I am able to see the effects the silence over the years has had. The reason my heart broke is because as with my mother, this is the story for many of the women in the world and also the women with whom I work. The common thread is that for years, women (we) have been silenced.

My inspiration came from knowing that we as women have come a long way from the times of keeping our truth silenced. I was inspired also because I have broken my generational pattern. Our matriarchal lineage begins in the wombs of our mothers and our mother's mother and beyond. Our beliefs and attitudes that we inhabit are literally handed down to us in the womb and by our parents. They are deeply embedded in our subconscious mind. Unless we are the ones to break these patterns, we will continue to carry them forward. These unconscious patterns become our core wounds in life, and often times, we have a mother and/or father wound. I work with women to heal their mother and father wound, their masculine/feminine wound, and whatever core wound you have. Healing our wounds is important if we want to step forward and shine.

Things that shape our lives such as personal habits, work, politics, and healthcare have been constructed with an absence of the feminine and with a distorted masculine. This is changing. There are many visible cracks in the patriarchal structures and large sections are crashing down. The light is pouring through. Women are extremely powerful and we are waking up and remembering the ways of the feminine. More and more of us are stepping into the Queen and or Priestess roles of our lives (more fun archetypal work). The rise of the Feminine is here and that means that more women are becoming leaders, speaking their truth, getting their needs meet, being expressed and sexpressed, being treated as equal, knowing and living their purpose and returning to the ways of the Feminine.

Sovereignty, Sexual Healing & Empowerment

Sovereignty

Crucial to finding your 'SHE' Spot is sovereignty. Sovereignty is full autonomy and self-rule by which you can have and create your life on your own terms guided and supported by your own ideals and values.

Sexual Healing & Empowerment

In October 2017, there was a **#metoo** famous tweet which is a social movement that went viral and encouraged every woman who had survived and was a victim of sexual harassment or assault to post their experience on Facebook and/or Twitter. It became a global movement. The **#metoo** movement raised a lot of awareness around the challenges that our culture and society face regarding sex and sexuality. Historically speaking, it is one of the most important topics brought forward, and mainstream. Its impact will definitely change the way men relate to women. Thank Goddess. Sex is one the most natural, incredibly pleasurable acts that we engage in as humans. Our sexuality is the most sacred thing we have. It is not necessarily about sex. It is a living, breathing, alive organism that changes throughout our lifetime and is unique to you. Our sexuality is a part of who we are and a part of us being whole.

There is a lot of stigma and taboo around sex and our sexuality. Shame, that which prevents us from being vulnerable, needs to be removed from ourselves. Vulnerability is about being real and authentic. We long for deep love, realness and authenticity. We also long for pleasure. It's our birthright. Desire is our yearning for this pleasure. The truth is that the desire for pleasure is the motivation behind all actions. Anything and everything aspired to and achieved produces a feeling of pleasure. Desire is ever present. It is with you with every step and every breath you take. Desire precedes your every action, since before you can do, you first have to want.

Our sex and sexuality are things that bring pleasure. The taboo around sex in our society is based on fear for what we don't understand. What we don't understand we make wrong or let have power over us. Some aspects to greater understanding of sex and our sexuality including removing shame are asking for what we need and healthy boundaries. Needs and having them met are critical in order for us to truly be satisfied, fulfilled and expressed.

Boundaries are also critical. Love cannot exist without them. Boundaries help you to set a clear understanding about what is important to you. They are rules and principles you live by that both people in the relationship discuss and agree to follow. If you don't set boundaries, guilt and resentment can settle in and can result in anger. If you feel resentful or victimized and are blaming someone or something, it might mean that you have not set healthy boundaries. Once you get practice setting boundaries, you feel empowered and suffer less anxiety, resentment, and guilt.

When you experience sexual healing and empowerment, you have more energy, feel healthier and happier, have true intimacy, feel more powerful in your body, in your business, and all your relationships. YES! You also have more confidence and magnetism and have the ability to manifest what you want through using your Sacred Feminine Energy.

Happiness

There is a thing called EROS, which is the river of energy that flows through us. There are many things that prevent that river from freely flowing in us. Let's take a look at a couple of them.

In today's society, women are juggling careers, relationships, family, and friends. As a result of this busyness, women have become burnt out, exhausted, overwhelmed and consequently function in man-mode. We are not meant to function in man-mode. Another result of the busyness is women are too tired for things that really matter: self-care, intimacy or time with loved ones. Sex becomes more of a task than for pleasure, and self-care is secondary. All are important for our happiness as are many things such as good health, being in nature, treating ourselves to that special something, owning our safety, knowing our needs, loving our bodies, changing our relationship to time, living our purpose, and having that special someone to share your life with. Because of the busyness, women have become shutdown and lose sight of the fact that our power as women lies in our Sacred Feminine Energy.

This Energy is life force energy. It is creative energy. Everything is energy! If you are shut down in your sexual center, you are shut down to your **FULL** power as a woman. It's important to give voice to your root. Your root voice speaks from your deepest feminine self. Whenever you feel lost, come back here to listen. She is strong. She is vital. She is the expression of your authentic woman. Ultimately to be happy, we have to do what gives us pleasure.

Extraordinary Love and Romantic Relationships

Love is why we are all here. Ask yourself this question? Am I in love? We need to love ourselves before we can truly love another. Are you in love? If you answered no, try to identify what shifts need to happen in your body, your mind, and where you are placing your energy and attention. What we focus on grows. The answer is more connection, not less. By being willing to do the work in our own intimate relationships, starting with ourselves and then our partners, we can begin doing the healing work for an entire population of women and men. The strength of the nation depends on the integrity of the home (self).

Extraordinary romantic relationships are those in which we are in for the right purpose and when we can stay deeply rooted and true to who we are and not abandon ourselves to be in partnership. Extraordinary romantic relationships are also when we take responsibility for our own actions and stop pointing the finger at the other person, when we understand our triggers and do not operate from them (emotional intelligence), when we have excellent communication skills and when we integrate sex and spirit.

When you have an extraordinary relationship, you feel more generous, more spaciousness, able to get your intimacy needs met at home, happier, more compassionate towards others, fulfilled, empowered in every other area of your life and you have the feeling like you can create something bigger than you can on your own.

My passion is helping women like you to stand in your **'SHE'** power, to manifest anything you want using your Sacred Feminine Energy, to feel safe and fully confident in and celebrating your body, knowing your purpose, needs and boundaries, to feel seen and heard, to balance love, family and career and to have the life, love & intimacy you truly desire.

Here are my 10 Tips to help you Embrace Your 'SHE':

1. Look into my *O'Bliss: Dream It, Birth It, Live It* course or my *Ignite Your Sacred Feminine Power* or *Jade Egg Alchemy & Initiation* Course.

2. Take time to meditate at least 10 minutes every day. Use the feminine form of meditation: bring your awareness down into the heart, belly and womb center.

3. Know that your body is a landing pad for your desires.

4. Move towards your fear. There really are only two fears: of falling and of loud noises. Everything else is learned.
5. Know your truth. We cannot lead others into the truth when we ourselves are not able to know our own truth.
6. Practice meaningful and care-Full communication
7. Shift how your being and your whole world will shift.
8. Face your shadow side. If you do not, you can never truly be alive or empowered because you will only living out one half of your existence.
9. Live your life through doing pleasure practices and practicing radical self-care.
10. Be in your feminine rhythm of life by using the cycles of the moon: first quarter, full moon, third quarter and new moon.

~Feminine Mojo, Find Your **'SHE'** Spot~

About the Author

I am a relationship, sexuality, and life coach, passionate about helping women live an embodied life of love, confidence, vitality, radiance, pleasure, and purpose. My desire is to teach you to create from your Sacred Feminine Power and Energy in a sustainable, joyful way in order to manifest and have what you want.

I work with women who feel that love has eluded them, who want deeper love, intimacy and connection, those who suffer from exhaustion, low libido, sex issues or difficulties with orgasm, who know that there is more to their love and sexuality than they have experienced, and those who want to live their purpose and prosper.

You deserve to have the legendary love that you want. You deserve to fully arrive – and thrive – within your magnificent, phenomenal female body, free of shame, pain or fear and feeling more confidence, courage, pleasure, and bliss in your life than ever before. Doing this will provide you with a new connection with yourself, your sexuality, and your relationships, as well as bring you to a new presence in your life and work. It can be the key that unlocks a new chapter of yourself and romantic love and personal expression that spills over into your life.

By embodying and accessing the FULL range of who you are, you will transform limiting and subconscious beliefs, fear, and trauma and cultivate sovereignty, self-trust, self-love and a profound sense of inner security and confidence that nourishes you throughout your life.

I infuse a diverse background of experiences to create an integrative approach to improving women's inner confidence, romantic and sex lives (whether you are single or partnered)

I work in-person and virtually.

Feminine Mojo, Find Your 'SHE' Spot: Partnership~ Prosperity~Pleasure~Purpose

Email: info@jennevieveybarra.com

Phone: (415) 940.3126

Website: jennevieveybarra.com

Facebook page: https://www.facebook.com/shespotjennevieve

Twitter: jennevieve@shespotcoach

Instagram: @shespotjennevieve

SECTION THREE

STEP INTO YOUR POWER AND PURPOSE.

Discover how to step more fully into your power as you step more fully into your purpose.

Your God is Bigger
Sarah Reilly, CNE, CNC

I was new here. I stood in the back row. A few hundred heads were bowed in this church, whispering prayers beneath their breath. Today's sermon continued to sink and swim in every cell of my body and so ensued an unwinding of long held, tethered silence I had kept.

Swallowing the lump in my throat, tears slipped through the corners of my eyes, following gravity's descent, along my cheeks, on to my sweat moistened chest and white tank top. It was a hot summer morning, and I had just entered this church after a brisk morning walk of feeding horses on the adjacent Iron Horse Trail. No tissue at hand. I never anticipated a meltdown in this new place that seemed welcoming and "interesting".

Opening my eyes amidst prayer; a tall, sturdy man to my right with his head in his hands; others with their heads bowed; some with their hands raised to the heavens singing along the profound response time music. This was a packed church auditorium of a few hundred. The soulful, elevating music stirred in me and I felt something heavy; a huge wave of heartache passing through my heart and every cell in my body. I began to crumble and cry. I grabbed the seat in front of me, losing my balance, humbled. A voice shot through me, speaking through me:

"You can no longer hide Sarah, this is bigger than you, and not about YOU". I have carried you this far, you know enough. You haven't been placed in this predicament to hide. It's time to step forward with what you know...what you have lived."

My heart ached, alligator tears, seeping a sorrow for those around me. I knew what they didn't know. They were innocent bystanders of a state bill called SB649. This bill was set to go to the Senate floor the following week. If passed, this bill would place 5G cell sites on residents' private property via light poles and utility poles, impeding right of way, property rights and most of all positioning a constant 5G Radiation into their homes...and they would NEVER have a right to turn it off. The plan of government and telecom industry was for them to never know about it. It would later be sold as a tagline for "improving the internet of all things and optimizing gap zones and connectivity". Not true.

There was a more horrific angle at work. **THE TRUTH**: 5G radiation had **not been** tested for human safety, nor in this type of proximity and duration of 24/7 exposure. However, 2G Radiation (a much lower radiation) has unequivocally proven to cause cancer, infertility, Alzheimer, Autism, inflammation and disorders of the brain, immune system, central nervous system and endocrine system.

These facts are irrefutable, yet this multi-billion-dollar telecommunications deal was in the works behind thick, shiny, closed doors on the Senate Floor.

I had just come privy to this bill the prior week and searched for media and press releases on it but couldn't find much of anything...this was a silent bill in the industry's back pocket that would soon be passed in California state wide and **NO ONE** would know!

That voice hit again...as the intensity of the music escalated. *"It's time to stop hiding Sarah, it's time."* I crumbled into a deep weeping; not only for this sadness of these residents, but for the mourning of "this self". **The mourning of "this self" I had held for years that could no longer hide. I was mourning her. The one who appeared to be "normal" on the outside, I had to let her go.** The one that kept this secret so everything looked ok on the surface and wasn't "judged", I had to let her go. The one who feared being doubted or ridiculed for a condition (as I had been in the past), I had to let her go. After all, I had to support myself and represent my business and make a living. I represent health and wellness. I had been warned, "Don't come out with your condition", it will pigeon hole you and no one will think that you can help them when you are dealing with something like that".

Again, the voice *"It's time to stop hiding and speak this truth."* **I broke down sobbing,** like a little girl in the corner with her blankie. I could not stop. The tears just - kept - coming; to the point I almost felt like I couldn't breathe anymore. *"Sarah, it is time for people to know this truth."* *"Yes"*, I thought to myself, as my hearted ached for these innocent, unknowing people, *"they need to know the truth and this must be stopped, SB649 must be stopped, but how?"* They had NO idea AND they would have NO right to speak out against it or take down the cell sites on their property EVER once installed. Was this truly America? The Land of the Free?

Stirred by this breaking down, a breakthrough would ensue. I went home that day to begin working on one of the first national press releases to go out in opposition to SB649. This press release was pointed to raise awareness across the country to all of the major newspapers and health reporters about this issue that would be going to the Senate floor in the next week in California. I worked around the clock to get this press release out on the cusp of the Senate vote. The voice that had been kept quiet for so long on this level, came forth like a roaring lion with such momentum, I almost couldn't find the words that blasted through me all at once, like a storm. I worked with a professional press release writer and seasoned activist in this issue to guide the finesse of this process. A higher force in the eleventh hour made this possible. No doubt.

The Backstory

Why was this issue so poignant for me? At the point of writing this, I have lived with Electro-sensitivity for the past 14 years. I have personally lived the implications of overexposure to wireless radiation. In 2003, I got wireless in my home amidst a steady stream of cell towers around my home. When I used Wi-Fi, I would have severe burning in my bones and tissues of my body with severe deep brain pain and it also affected my breathing and heart. Soon, I would become sensitive to all other forms of EMF's as well from voltage, lights, sunlight, etc. Most doctors passed it off as a fluke of symptoms. I spent 5 years living in an isolated manner just to survive and continue healing.

This "knowing" about these frequencies of 2G-5G has whirled inside me for years. My knowing comes from the fact I had to dig for the truth. As I became Electro-sensitive in 2003, all of my symptoms would become so severe to the point they were debilitating and extremely isolating as the world became more saturated with these frequencies. I began my personal quest to make my pain go away and learn WHY Wi-Fi, cell phones and cordless phones caused this burning, deep bone and brain pain. I spent years and tens of thousands of dollars to get to the bottom of this. I researched and talked to scientists and doctors around the world and learned that what we are exposed to in the realm of wireless technology is insufficiently tested for human safety. How could this be true if we are told in the United States that it is safe? Here is why:

Myth vs. Truth

This technology is strongly enabled through federal laws of commerce governed by the FCC. The FCC is "The Federal Communications Commission". It is an independent agency of the United States government created by statute to regulate interstate communications by radio, television, wire, satellite, and cable. Telecomm industry says this wireless radiation technology is safe because it meets FCC Requirements. The standard response from industry to health concerns from wireless technology such as Wi-Fi routers, cell phones, cell towers, smart meters, cordless phones, baby monitors and now small cells on utility poles is the following: *"It meets the FCC Guidelines, therefore it does not pose a health hazard"*. However, there is a critical glitch with this statement.

Here it is:

1. OUTDATED-FCC/TELECOMM GUIDELINES
    a. FCC Regulations are outdated based on old technology. They were established in the mid 1990's and technology has exponentially evolved. They have not been updated since!
2. THERMAL vs. NON-THERMAL
    a. The FCC Regulations are based on a radiation that has IONIZING "THERMAL AFFECTS" (tissue heating).
    b. Wireless radiation (from cell towers, cell phones, Wi-Fi, etc) is NON-IONIZING "NON-THERMAL."
    c. The fact they claim the technology meets FCC "Thermal" requirements says nothing whether or not there is any risk associated with the exposure of non-thermal radiation because they are comparing apples and oranges.

What we DO know is that the scientific proof of health consequences is irrefutable:

- Over 2,000 published research studies prove biological impact from non-thermal RFR.
- 180 scientists are calling for a moratorium on 5 G and small cells based on the science.
- The $25 million National Toxicology Program Study conducted by the NIH observed an increase in brain tumors (gliomas) and malignant schwann cell tumors of the heart and that, exposure to 2G RFR [radio frequency radiation] has the potential to induce

measurable DNA damage under certain exposure conditions." This study confirmed, "clear evidence" of cancer. Rats exposed to these frequencies had DNA changes in:

- in the frontal cortex
- in peripheral leukocytes
- in the hippocampus
- Ronald L. Melnick, PhD, the NIH toxicologist who lead the NTP study design and senior advisor to the Environmental Health Trust states: "For children the cancer risks may be greater than that for adults because of greater penetration and absorption of cell phone radiation in the brains of children and because the developing nervous system of children is more susceptible to tissue-damaging agents.
- This study was done at 2G. Frequencies proposed for cell sites is exponentially higher at 4G, which will soon evolve to 5G (if not stopped for due diligence of 3rd party testing for human safety).

- Other health correlations are
- Autism
- Alzheimer's
- Infertility
- Damage to fetuses
- Disorders of the immune system, central nervous system, endocrine system, reproductive system.

The Persistent Giant

SB649 did pass the Senate Floor, before it went to the Assembly in a few months. Over this time, there was a collective up swell of activism against this bill. It passed Assembly, however many in the office had been swayed during this time of up swell. Next stop was the Governor's desk. Would he sign it or veto it? The bill sat on his desk until the 11th hour when he eventually vetoed it. It was a victorious celebration. However, two federal bills are in the wake of this veto that are looking to pass 5G in an accelerated roll out if not stopped, so the work continues of activists and interest groups who are privy to this.

Your God, YOUR Power

You must know that corporate interest trumps human welfare; 'Period.' I wish it wasn't the case, however I have done 16 years of research on both environmental toxin exposure of wireless radiation AND chemicals/toxins in our environment. Industry is ALWAYS out for their bottom line and will make it look otherwise. We are not protected.

Whether it's the FCC, USDA or FDA; 'We' truly have to be conscious consumers and do our homework. Know that your voice, your calling and truth matter; your voice and stepping forward can make a difference, no matter how big the giant is that you are taking on. I would have not known about this had I not had my own personal circumstance.

Here is what I learned about taking a stand and being willing to shine the truth:

1. When you feel a swell of truth in your heart, surrender to it and speak it.
2. Deeply envision your desired outcome amidst intentional prayer.
3. Engage with others who have expertise in your goal.
4. Keep going even when it feels impossible.
5. Surrender to the grace of God, the greater universal force that inextricably connects us all.

For those who want to learn more about how to be wireless wise, here are a few immediate tips where you can take action:

Top 3 Tips to be Wireless Wise

1. Don't hold a cell phone to your head EVER (Especially when it is ringing or has low bars). Always use speaker or headphones and keep away from your body.
2. Put it on 'airplane' when you put it by your bedside as an alarm.
3. Don't carry it adjacent to your body while it is on. Keep it at a distance from your body in a purse, backpack, etc. Ideally, turn off or put on airplane if carrying it adjacent to your body.

For more tips go to www.getnourished.net/emfdetox

About the Author

Sarah Reilly is a Functional Nutritionist, Speaker and Radio Show Host. She is a trusted international leader in functional nutrition serving clients across the country. She is a *Burn Out/Recovery Specialist* who helps burnt out business leaders, athletes, and those with complex conditions to recover, rebuild and achieve peak performance. As a Functional Nutritionist, she combines principles of Holistic Nutrition and Functional Medicine to help her clients get to the root cause of fatigue, pain, digestive issues and stubborn weight so they can get turned back on in their body, life AND mission again.

For the last 15 years; Sarah has studied Nutrition and Functional Medicine and has traveled the world to work personally with the global leaders in Functional-Neurology, Clinical-Nutrition, Functional-Medicine, Homeopathy and Ayurveda. Birthed from her own determination to resolve her painful symptoms of Electro-sensitivity (ES), Sarah has researched the physiological impacts of electromagnetic fields and wireless radiation for the last 16 years.

This has enabled her to progressively heal from ES while serving as a steward of awareness to others of how to protect themselves from overexposure to wireless radiation in their daily life and to help the up swell of individuals emerging with ES due to overexposure. Sarah has also been an integral activist in efforts on the local and state level to push back aggressive rollouts of dangerously high wireless radiating technology in close proximity to living environments.

Sarah runs her private virtual nutrition practice, called Get Nourished, which serves clients nationally.

Email: sarah@getnourished.net

Phone: 415-419-4490 Website: www.getnourished.net

Facebook: www.facebook.com/getnourished.net

LinkedIn: www.linkedin.com/in/sarah-reilly-nutritionist

Twitter: www.twitter.com/getnourished

It's All About Your Attitude
Sean Sullivan

What helps me stand out and succeed is forcing and giving myself no choice but to be motivated from within! I will say it again what helps me stand out and succeed is forcing and giving myself no choice but to be motivated from within!! I have a disability called Autism that causes me to stand out and be seen differently and frequently treaded differently…and unfortunately poorly at times. It has also led me on my own hero's journey.

An example of this is I was at a boarding school (Crater Lake School) during my six months to a year and a half stay there I was forced to sleep outside with no covers and no pillow. This happened each night this alone was extremely tough and hard to endure to make everything even more frustrating **I was the only one who was made to do this! In the beginning I would ask the staff why? Why do I have to do to do this? The staff would answer by punching me in the stomach and saying** *"anymore questions?"* Going forward, I knew that this was going to be a gigantic test of endurance. I write only some of what I endured because that was just barely the beginning of my torments! Not just the staff but also the students would get pleasure and enjoyments in seeing me suffer and be in agony! I asked myself: *"Is it not enough that I am the only student that is forced to sleep outside with nothing but my clothes to help me stay worm? I asked myself why? Why are the students, the faculty and the administration making me the only one to sweep the floors, making me the only one to mop and only giving me breakfast when there were leftovers, only giving me lunch when there were leftovers and the same for dinner!"*

Often there were no leftovers so I did not get to eat and when I did get to eat I was forced to eat outside! For the longest time, I had truly believed that it was my fault, that I did something wrong, that I did something to deserve this trial! To make matters even worse I had to keep my feelings of resentment, anguish, sadness and self-pity to myself because if I shared my feelings and thoughts than it would be at great cost and also because there was no one absolutely no one who had any not even a shred of humanity, respect and kindness! I simply thought that I was having a never-ending nightmare and or I was in a horror show!!!! During my time at that awful place I would make the attempt countless times to run away and each time I was taken back by the police! Until one time I was taken to a Juvenile Hall! This most likely happened to teach me that I am powerless and no one will help me nor will anyone care about me!!!!!

Finally, some good news happened. Somehow the police discovered what was happening. To this day I do not have the slightest idea how! It couldn't have been any of the other students because they were treated like royalty compared to me. They even got to go out in the community I did not, they got a perfect temperature shower, I got what was left which was almost always freezing cold and I was not allowed to use the phone. The police found out, but somehow, the school found out that the police had found out so they took all of us including me to try and conceal what was really going on! They took us from the school in Oregon to an island in Washington State! This trip's two main objectives were to at all costs not be shut down and to make it very, very hard for me to expose them!

Fortunately for me I found a kayak and so I immediately without thinking got in the kayak with no life jacket and no previous training left the island and the school. I then preceded to kayak for about 6 miles! I could see the Space Needle and all I could think about was getting to Seattle. The trouble was, when I finally go to Seattle. I had no idea where the police station was! However, I did see a Highway so I went to the highway and pretended like I was a cheerleader in hopes that someone would call the police.

Someone did. The police arrived and I told them everything. The police took me to a waiting area that had a place for me to sleep on an actual bed with real live covers pillows and everything. **I could not believe my eyes. I could not believe that something good, something great, something amazing was at last at long last happening to me!**

That is how I perceived the situation at the time because of all the bad, all the nefarious things and acts that I have been through. I was used to people harming me and treating me poorly. It felt like an eternity! So, when something that a whole lot of people consider normal, having a bed with pillow a pillow and cover, having my own meal, and kindness…it was a lot to absorb.

I had begun to think both consciously and unconsciously that this is the life, not that this is what I deserve and am entitled to! As I continued to wait for my mom to fly from New Jersey to Seattle to come and get me I continued to live and relive everything that I had been, what it taught me, the lessons I learned from living through and surviving those experiences!

The sad part was at first, that I did not learn anything accept being angry. Eventually, I discovered meditation. I learned to take a whole lot of deep breaths, meditated and calmed myself down! After I did that which was quite surprisingly easy then and only then was I able to think clearly. **When I thought clearly, I truly realized that none of it, none of the horrors, none of the humiliations and none of the torments was my fault!** None of the many times that people threw rocks at me was my fault; zero percent of it all is my fault! After I realized this truth, the next phase of my training happened: **Which was thinking to myself what exactly was it that got me through this ordeal? Was it merely a coincidence? Or was it because I have an endless amount of internal motivation and a refusal attitude to allow the terrible situation to defeat me?** This has led me to the advice I want to share with you:" Never let bad situations conquer you in any way!!" (You can use me as an example if you want!)

I went through pure horror and I'm still here. During this time, I also almost died from a very bad asthma attack, was in a 10-day coma, on life support, ended up needing physical and occupational therapy. Yet, I'm still hear and committed to making a positive difference for others.

Remember that you are your own author every choice you make, every action you take is a deciding factor in whether your unique story will be a best seller or not! You and you alone can forge a path! "If there is no path make one, if there is an obstacle destroy or choose to overcome the obstacle!!"

I do not have time for doubts to enter my mind and neither should you. I think that the main reason why this is the way I think is because of my unlimited passion, drive and determination to prove to myself and others. Just because I have a disability, which is autism, by no means does that mean does that justify me just throwing in the towel and giving up. Well, I don't settle for *"I tried what more do you want?"* Sorry but "no" not in a billion years as long as I am alive, as long as there is breath in me. I will keep fighting and fighting until I win, until I succeed! This attitude, of being committed to succeeding…never giving up, is the attitude that I have regarding my life. 'ITT,' is the attitude that I will continue to have forever!!!

This is the attitude that I want to pass on to you. You can choose to never give up…to not settle and to commit to your success. No one else can do it for you. Here are my tips to help you Step Forward and SHINE…no matter what challenges may come:

- Keep going no matter what.
- No matter the challenge, you can choose your attitude.
- We are all worthy of good treatment, remember to treat others and yourself well.
- Sometimes we have to be willing to rescue ourselves.
- Remember to pause and breathe
- Choose to forgive.
- Choose gratitude and love.

Become passionate about creating your own path, writing your own story, and choosing to step forward and SHINE! Remember, you are the author of your own story and life. Choose to SHINE!

About the Author

Hi, my name is Sean Sullivan; I am an individual who has Autism Spectrum Disorder. Growing with autism has been very hard and tiring, it has made it very hard for me to make friends, my fellow peers if you can call them that would get pleasure and enjoyment in teasing, making fun of me and even hurting me physically! I enjoy watching anime, which is, Japanese cartoons.

One of my favorite anime are Naruto, which is about an orphaned boy who everyone hates because of a fantasy not real demon attacking his village killing a lot of people including his parents and then the demon was sealed with in Naruto! As the story progresses we find out that Naruto is desperately working and trying to gain peoples approval and friendship!!

I also enjoy eating at nice restaurants, such as the Queen Mary which requires both, a reservation as well as suit and tie! Another enjoyment of mine is improving my website, making additions to it such as adding YouTube videos as well as replying to comments. My website is one of the very few things I take true pride in and take very seriously! Maybe that is why my website is the first result on the first page of Google!

(949) 514-5720

seaniknowautism@gmail.com

iknowautism.org

https://www.facebook.com/IKNOWAUTISM.org

https://www.facebook.com/sean.sullvan

https://www.youtube.com/channel/UCV5iA8xzVgZjnsOStNcgTHw

https://plus.google.com/u/0/102578198097930653877

Connect To Your Heart
(Trust Your Higher Self)
Phyllis Flemings, PhD

Do you feel that there is something that you were born to do but don't know how? Have others told you that you were great at doing a certain thing and you figured that what you did was no important thing and they were just being nice? Is there a burning desire in your heart right now and you are just putting it to the side knowing that you don't have time to learn anything new plus it would be entirely too hard to learn the steps? Well many of us have had some of those thoughts and have attempted to let them fly away or at least hoped that they would fly away. Most times though they just come back until we act.

I am familiar with asking myself some of these questions and trying to act by just sticking my toe in the water hoping that would be enough. Unfortunately, the toe in the water just won't work. The questions keep coming and they get louder and louder demanding your attention. **You eventually will need to give them the attention that they require.**

As a young child, I loved working with people. I enjoyed acting in plays, speaking before groups and teaching. I was able to see another side of a challenge that could make a difference; I was able to help others see a different point of view that would be more uplifting and would bring them joy. Doing this also brought me joy and I continued to learn, grow, teach and coach. I did not choose the field of teaching and coaching at the time but continued to do it because I found it helpful to me and to others. Later I did become a teacher and a Certified Coach.

It is amazing how those questions keep coming up reminding us that we have a gift and we need to take massive action and share that gift on a larger scale. HOW DO WE DO THAT? We ask ourselves. We don't have a clue what steps to take and we really don't think that what we do is a big deal. **We just know that we love people and we want to support them in any way that we can.**

THE CALLING

I had a wonderful job **in the public sector** and worked with a group of awesome people. We were all able to share our ideas and we learned a lot from each other. I was able to coach and teach in a very supportive environment even thought my job was to lead and manage. As I moved forward in my career, I felt that I was doing what I loved and making a difference. I came to a point where I was eligible to retire, and the voice became very clear that it was time for me to share my message with more people: It was time for me to take massive action. I was so convinced that I did retire and stepped out to live my passions and follow my bliss. Having an intention was great AND knowing what action to take was even better. This is where I had some learning to do. I needed to discover what actions I needed to take to build what I was called to build and be who I was called to become.

MISTAKES

I'm hoping in sharing some of my mistakes and discoveries, I can help you move forward powerfully in your life…and hopefully not make some of the mistakes I made. **I didn't ask for help and instead attended seminar after seminar and took course after course.** I did not ask for help for I felt that I had made the decision and needed to make it happen on my own. That was the second mistake and the first being that I didn't have a plan before I decided to retire. It would be great if those were the only miss-steps that I made but there were more to follow. You have heard that the definition of insanity is doing the same thing over and over and expecting different results. Well, I kept taking more classes, getting more knowledge and not taking the action that I needed to take. A third mistake, not being clear and having a plan and the fourth was not taking action. To be less harsh and a little kinder, *I admit that it would have been almost impossible for me to act when I had no plan.*

I have discovered the good news that you can stop and build a plan at any time to move forward. It is never too late to build a plan.

There were other things that I needed to do before making my dream of helping others come true. I am grateful that I was able to realize what I needed to do before giving up. (Feeling that I was not the person to make that difference that I felt called to make.) Fortunately for me, I came to myself as the prodigal son did, and made the decision to get clear, set my intention, give my intention, attention, and let go. I needed to create a plan then take clear and inspired action.

Once I got clear and knew what I needed to do, things began to happen. Once I was honest with myself and was willing to ask for help, things started to move forward. By going through struggle and what I considered as failure (which was really lessons that I learned) I was truly able to claim the position of an authentic messenger, here to support others in moving forward with clarity and ease.

I am now a Transformational Life Coach who believes that we all can live a passionate life. I support people in discovering or rediscovering their passions and making sure that those passions are in their life. I help them get clear and know what they love and what is important to them. If you are working and you enjoy what you do, continue to do that work and add other things into your life that you are passionate about. We are all here for a purpose and we all have something to offer. If we don't yet know what that is, we can sit quietly in a place without distractions and ASK. Ask the "what" and the "how" ...and the next step so that we can develop a plan to bring passion into your life.

If you are skilled at something, have something that you enjoy doing, feel within your heart that there is an opening that needs to be filled, **then, I want to share with you IT IS TIME to do what you desire to do.** Know that if you were not capable of doing the thing that keeps coming up for you to do, you would not have the desire to do it. We are all given certain talents and when we connect with our heart, we can know what they are.

If you are ready to take that step forward toward bringing your passion(s) forward, then here are my suggestions to help you Step Forward and SHINE!

Take some time to sit quietly and ask your heart to tell you what you should do and how you can get started;

Get clarity by making a list of the things that you enjoy doing or have a Passion Facilitator help you discover or rediscover your passions;

Pick the top five things that you love and are passionate about and give those things your attention daily so that they will become a part of who you are because now that you have these passions, you must set your intention to live them;

Every day take time to look at your list, congratulate yourself on your follow through and be grateful for the day and EVERYTHING that has happened that day. Do not judge whether you felt it was good or bad just know that you are being moved forward to your good because you have set your intentions and you are giving those intentions, attention;

Develop your plan, your blueprint, of how you want things to work and trust that they will work. Get support and help with developing your plan. Remember that what you desire to do for good, you can do, otherwise you would not have that desire;

Don't be afraid to ask for help when you need it. Get an accountability partner who will support you and help keep you on track as you move forward;

Find a daily ritual that supports you. Here are some ideas of daily practices that could work for you: Prayer, meditation, inspirational reading, inspirational audios or videos, journal writing, gratitude lists, affirmations, stretching and many other things that you can do. You want to be consistent and persistent so that you will know that you are serious about making the difference that you desire to make and are committed to supporting yourself as you move forward. You want your subconscious to be programmed in supporting your dreams.

Our journey can be so much more enjoyable when we check in and remember to do what we love. I want you to live with clarity, focus, ease and grace. I want our lives to be passionate and on purpose.

We have things to do and only so much time to get those things done. We are all connected, and we are available to support each other because by doing what we love, we can make a significant difference not only in our family, our community, our city, our state, or our nation. You can make a difference in the world by saying "yes" and moving into your calling. I look back on what I called struggles and failures and can be grateful for all of them because I have learned so much and all of that made me the person that I am now, and I am feeling better and better about that person. **Once you get clear, set your intentions, take action by giving them attention, you will notice a change in your life.**

Be grateful knowing that you are moving in the right direction. By taking small steps towards what you want, you are making a difference. We don't always know how many people we touch by just doing what we do BUT know you are making a difference.

If I were to speak to my younger self who was slow about doing what she loved, I would tell her the same things that I am telling you. Know that you already have everything that you need within you to be, do, and have the life that you want, and you can do whatever you desire. Never give up on your passions or your dreams and always stay connected to your heart for if you listen, it will always lead you in the right direction. Be confident, be determined, and be patient.

Quotes:

Know that you are enough.

You have everything that you need within you.

Be grateful for everything for you don't know what seed of greatness exists.

Be kind, compassionate, and loving.

Love is always the answer.

"What you appreciate, appreciates". Lynne Twist

"You are not a drop in the ocean, you are the entire ocean in a drop".
Rumi

I believe in you and look forward to seeing you step forward and SHINE!

About the Author

Dr. Phyllis Flemings is a Transformational Passionate Living Coach who helps people discover or rediscover who they are and revitalize those passions that may be hidden. She has an MPA in Public Administration and a PhD in Metaphysics. She also has numerous certifications in various fields to include coaching and passion facilitation.

Phyllis has over 30 years leading, training, and coaching others to live their passions knowing that by doing so, their lives will be filled with clarity, focus, ease and grace. She supports them in realizing their purpose.

Dr. Flemings is a co-author in three Anthologies where she talks about her life and how others can live their life with more joy, passion and purpose leading them to offering their wonderful gifts to others - to really make a difference in the world that only they can make. Her primary focus is on love knowing that love is the great connector with all people and once we love ourselves and then others, we can do remarkable things together. Dr. Flemings is the founder of 'Phoenix Rising Again' a training and coaching organization. To arrange a complementary strategy session with her, please call 707-688-9097.

Phoenixrising197@gmail.com

1-707-688-9097

www.phyllisflemings.com

Facebook: Phoenix Rising Again

LinkedIn: Phyllis Flemings

Twitter: @PAFRAF

Unleash Your Possibility
Mary E. Knippel

"I dwell in possibility," the poet Emily Dickinson tells us. How beautiful to look at life that way. A world is filled with wonder and awe.

The poem also speaks about Paradise. How wonderful to possibly create your own paradise. And I believe you can. You have the power to do just that.

I believe we are born innocents with all this possibility in front of us. Then we grow up and become afraid that we aren't enough. That we will never measure up to the accomplishments of others. Thus, we decide that the answer is to play it safe and silent. To live invisible and small.

I encourage you to step out of the shadow. Step into the light of your own brilliance. Shine and be seen for the gift you are to this world.

Let yourself experience what is possible for you. Be curious about those fleeting thoughts that you dismiss so readily because your inner critic challenges you by asking, "how could you possibly do that?"

What if Grandma Moses had never revisited her childhood dream of painting? That wasn't a skill she suddenly began at the age of seventy-eight, art had always been a part of her life.

What if Amelia Earhart gave up being a woman willing to break out of traditional roles?

What if a little girl born in poverty in rural Mississippi never took her ad-lib talents into the talk show arena to become the phenomenon we know as Oprah Winfrey?

While certain times of your life can give pause: a milestone birthday, a significant anniversary, the death of someone close to you, an accident or a catastrophic illness. It takes something really big in your life to have us take some sort of action and make changes. In my case, I thought I was pretty content leading the life I had always dreamed of having. My husband had a good job and provided a beautiful life for us. We had adopted a sweet baby girl and we were a family. I had achieved my goal of earning a college degree and even worked part time as an Editorial Assistant for a monthly newspaper. I'd weathered some major life transitions and even coped pretty will with uprooting our family twice.

Then that form letter arrived. The form letter that said I had an abnormal mammogram and my life was never the same again.

With my first breast cancer diagnosis and surgery, I threw myself back into my normal routine as quickly as I could. I believe that I wanted to pretend that first diagnosis never happened.

Three years later the second diagnosis and the time surgery were scheduled, I thought I was coping very well. I was so matter of fact about it that I scheduled a world tour after the procedure. Well, not exactly a world tour, although with all the logistics and planning it felt monumental. I treated the procedure it as if I was going in for a teeth cleaning instead of the second breast cancer outpatient surgery.

However, the day before my surgery, I had a violent attack of vertigo. If you have never experienced vertigo. It feels like a non-stop Tilt-a-Whirl ride. A constant spinning with no one there to turn off the whirling. On the surface, I seemed to be calmly conducting business as usual, but apparently my insides were spinning out of control necessitating a trip to the ER. And travel anywhere was not an option.

I was forced to stop and pause. My physical world and my inner world demanded that I pay attention. Has that ever happened to you? Was there ever a time where you ignored whispers to slow down, take a breath or linger a while? And the more you pushed through to try and "make it happen" you became upset and frustrated that what you wanted to have happen was not happening. The whisper turned into a howling that would not go away until you paid attention. That nagging feeling of something important will not be put off. And life as you know it changes in an instant.

I woke up to the all the possibility in my life after my second surgery. I saw all the ways I was playing it safe and being invisible.

No longer content to be shy and quiet Mary, who went along with whatever others decided. I stepped in to leadership roles in the clubs and organizations I participated in. I sought out ways to contribute my skills by volunteering to write articles and use my creativity on the newsletter or fundraising projects. Using my experience as a journalist, I started speaking and facilitating workshops focusing on the importance of your story. I was willing to step forward and share more of my voice and message and help others do the same. Where are you perhaps hiding…playing it safe? Where can you step out a little bit more sharing more of you and your gifts? Mine was in writing, leadership roles, speaking and helping others. You must decide what is right for you and take action

I am on a mission now to encourage everyone not to wait until they have a health crisis of their own to make changes. Life is too short to wait. The statistics say one in eight women will be diagnosed in her lifetime with breast cancer. **Don't wait to be a statistic to step forward and choose to shine in your own life. You are too important and what you have to offer is too valuable and needed to wait.**

Give yourself permission to follow your dreams. Plot a new path for yourself. You are worth it. No one else has your gifts. The gifts you alone can share with the world.

Let's stop and take a breath here. I realize that my suggestion may sound daunting to plot a new path for you. Honestly, you have all the tools necessary to discover whatever is the next steps are for you. In fact, I can share a powerful way to help you discover your new path. It's easier than you think and in fact something I've been doing since I was eleven years-old. You have probably dabbled in this activity at times too. Want to know what that mysterious suggestion could be? It's start writing in a journal. You can bring your dreams to life and journaling is the path to get there by capturing it on paper.

The most valuable advice I can share with you is to pick up a pen and write (longhand) in a journal. It's the most incredible tool to be able to connect your heart with your head and literally see your thoughts on the page. **Whether you ever want to share those words with the world, it is important that YOU gain the insights and wisdom of your inner knowing.** Your journal is a refuge, resource and record of your life. It can help you focus, keep you grounded, and not only remind you where you've been; it is a vehicle to propel you forward.

Just the way some have a meditation practice or a yoga practice, I encourage every woman to have a writing practice. Spend time alone with your journal every day. Pick a time you can show up consistently and block out time on your calendar just for you and your journal. It doesn't have to be long; five to fifteen minutes will allow you to establish a writing practice. Choose a pretty notebook and a fast-writing pen. Always put the date and time at the top of the page. Describe your surroundings to ground yourself in time and space. Set the timer and go. Keep your pen moving until the timer goes off.

Unleash the writer in you. There is someone out there waiting to hear from you. Someone you are meant to impact by sharing the story only you can share. I firmly believe we all have a message for the world only we can deliver. And if we don't share that message, someone else will not have the distinctive life experience they were destined to have. Take dictation from your soul and turn off the inner critic who is telling you this is a waste of time. Do not listen to the task-master who is nagging you to get busy with your To-Do list.

Just write!

Your possibilities are waiting for you! Your life is a wonder and wonderful. A journal will help you document the awe and wonder of your day-to-day experience. Everything that has happened in your life has made you who you are today. A journal can help you explore and go deeper into you uncovering your gifts and sharing them with the world.

To help you get started, please go to:

https://yourwritingmentor.com/2016jgift/ to download a journal I've created for you with some of my favorite inspirational quotes. Remember, you have all the wisdom inside of you, the words are ready…it's time for you to give them a voice!

My message to you is to not wait. <u>Step forward into your life now and go after whatever it is you have a passion to pursue</u>. Step up to believing in yourself. Step out of the shadow and shine as the gift you are to the world.

Claim your own Paradise. Discover your own possibility in which to dwell.

About the Author

Best-selling author Mary E. Knippel, Writer Unleashed at YourWritingMentor.com, publisher at Authentic Grace Publishing and inspirational speaker, is fiercely committed to guiding you to unleash your story worth writing. With a firm philosophy that *No one can tell your story but YOU*, Mary invites you to take pen in hand to deliver your expertise to the world. Using her 30 years as a journalist, and the power of storytelling, she is on a mission to support you to be visible, vibrant and prosperous. Someone is waiting to hear your story…the story only you can tell.

As a journal writer since the age of 11, Mary knows the enormous power and healing capabilities of the written word. A two-time breast cancer survivor, she used writing and other creative tools in her recovery and chronicles the results in her upcoming book, *The Secret Artist*, where she shares what she has learned to help you move from survive to thrive. Learn more about Mary's virtual classes and workshops, receive free writing tips and techniques as well as what to do about writer's block, or invite her to speak to your group, by visiting her website at:

www.yourwritingmentor.com.

mary@yourwritingmentor.com
650-440-5616

http://yourwritingmentor.com
https://facebook.com/maryeknippel.author

https://facebook.com/maryeknippel

https://www.linkedin.com/in/maryeknippel/

https://twitter.com/MEKnippelAuthor

https://www.youtube.com/user/maryeknippel

Clear the Clutter and SHINE!
Holly Porter

We all have clutter in our life—the crap, time zappers, and non-productive activities. In this chapter, you will discover how clearing my clutter has made a difference for me to move forward and shine, and also how it can help you. Jokingly, I always say, "I can share with you everything not to do," and there is much truth in that statement. Life is all about the lessons you've learned, and from those lessons, you will gain true success. At the very least, the lessons can be a helpful guide to a successful path.

Have you ever noticed someone when they walk in a room and it lights up? Have you ever noticed when someone walks into the room and it feels dim or heavy? My goal after you read this is to show you how to be the light, so when you walk in a room you light it up!

Here are a few strategies that help me clear the clutter and shine. Remember, any change can be easy; it is us who makes it hard.

Set Clear Intentions.

Be very specific on what you want. Have you heard the saying, "Be careful what you wish for, you just might get it?" Manifestation is a powerful source. Your mind can create anything you desire.

I had a friend who once shared a funny story with me (not funny to her). She wanted to manifest a family man, and soon she began dating this great guy. Everything was going perfectly, then at about six months into the relationship she found out he was married and already had children! She got a family man alright! She forgot to be specific that she wanted a man who was single with the desire to be a family man. Be specific and clear when setting intentions…I can't say that enough.

My mind moves too quickly to meditate for too long; however, I have created a 10-minute morning ritual to help. In just 10 minutes you can do energy clearing, affirmations, and a short meditation/prayer. When I put this into practice, the results are unbelievable! A couple years ago I was able to manifest a large sum of money in my real estate company. I did some visualizations of what I needed and **POW**, just like that I had more closings in a month than ever, and it was December, the slowest month of the year! Another time when I was younger, I saw these beige corduroy boots pictured in a magazine that I loved. I cut it out and put onto a vision board. I found it about twenty years later in an old box. As I looked it over, I realized I had a pair of those exact boots in the picture I had cut out, and put onto the board.

Manifesting is a powerful thing and if you are lacking in those skills, we should connect!

Here are some important tips when you are doing energy clearing and setting intentions:

Be open to the universe giving you what you're asking for. Again, be specific, and ready for other ways to receive what you're asking for. For example, when I was looking for financial gain I began saying affirmations and practicing visualizations. The money started showing up in my real estate business, not my coaching business. The universe does not differentiate where it comes from, if you're open to receive, it may come from the easiest source. I happen to have some listings which went under contract and then buyers showed up. This happened in December, which is usually the slowest month of the year; but, for me, it ended up being the biggest month I had in twelve years!

My husband, seeing me so excited about my experience, shared "I don't know what you're doing, but keep doing it!"

Start with simple things, and work up to the hard things

You can't run a marathon until you learn to run a mile. If you play too big while you're learning something in the beginning, you will get discouraged and be more likely to fail. No one sets out to fail. Have an end game plan. Start with the end-result you want; then work backwards to the beginning. Then take the steps to bring your desired outcome forward.

15 BEST PRACTICES FOR LIFE AND BUSINESS

Now for the real secret sauce! Fifteen best practices I have learned to implement, and by following these, you will be on top of business and life.

1. **Clean out the clutter in your life.** Do what I call, "Clean House." Clean house with your home, your friends, and anything that is

not in harmony with the direction you are headed. If it isn't serving you, get rid of it!

2. **Keep your desk and counters free of extra papers and stuff.** It is hard to focus when your surroundings are a cluttered mess.

3. **Use the 3D-System.** Do it, Delegate it, or Delete it. This system gives you three choices of what to do every day to remove tasks off your to-do list. By the end of each day, the list is gone; because, you did it, delegated it to someone else, or you deleted it—either permanently or for the day. Create a filing system with a folder for each day of the week. Organize each task for each day into two categories:

1. Trivial Many

2. Critical Few

The Trivial Many tasks, are all the things you do in your day that really don't matter as much; but, they make you feel like you have crossed off a lot on your to-do list.

Critical few are the tasks that are most important (ranking the highest priority); but, they usually take the longest and aren't as much fun to do. Your goal is to put the Critical Few first on your list to get them over with. Be careful not to sabotage your own success. Make a list that is doable.

1. **Outsource.** You cannot be everything to everyone; so, delegate tasks to those who have more expertise than you. (Enlace, Fivver, Odesk, Freelancer, or local college students are great for this.) Once you begin to delegate tasks, you can spend more time in your genius zone and on your MMAs (Money Making Activities).

2. **Separate personal and business time.** I know, I know, with technology making it easy to work while you play (especially for those who have a laptop lifestyle), you still need time to wind down and enjoy your loved ones.

3. **Self-care.** (This should probably have been #1 on this list.) If you don't take care of you, you are not going to be great for anyone else! Maybe it's something simple like a bubble bath, a walk in the park, dinner with friends, or reading. Figure out what self-care looks like for you, and make sure you do plenty of it!

4. **Quiet your mind.** Do this by allowing yourself to have some thinking time and private time. One idea for you to implement is to put a STOP sign on your door for others to see and know that

you are currently unavailable. Make sure your phone is on vibrate… or better yet, off. During this time, take a few minutes to breathe, meditate, or catch a power nap. Once you are refreshed and ready to be accessible to others again, be sure to turn your phone back on to the normal settings.

5. **Strive to focus on one project at a time.** It is too easy today to multitask. Funny thing is, we tend to believe we are good at it. STOP! It is just confusing your mind. If you are like me, and find yourself saying "focus, focus, focus" all the time, then you know it is time to slow down, stop multitasking, and take a break!

6. **Do periodic self-check-ins**. Ask yourself questions like: *Am I using my time wisely? Could I do this differently? Is there a better way to get this done?*

7. **Have boundaries.** In a world of *quick and easy* and *immediate gratification,* set boundaries for all who pull at your coattail. Have a set time when you will be on social media, check your emails, and return phone calls. Otherwise, others will highjack your time, and before you know it, the day is over!

8. **Schedule work** (or those Critical Few tasks), during your prime time—the time of day when you tend to accomplish the most and are the most productive. (My prime time is 10am-2pm.) I often jokingly tell my husband, "Sorry you missed it!"

9. **Take breaks throughout the day.** Walk around a little, stretch your legs, go up and down some stairs, and stay hydrated. Taking much needed breaks during the day will increase your focus and productivity.

10. **Set alarms for meetings and tasks that you don't want to forget.** This way you are not looking at the clock all day, wondering if it's time for something. Make sure it's a different ring tone than everything else, so it is sure to capture your attention.

11. **Create a reward system for yourself.** (Whatever that looks like for you.) Celebrate life and everything you accomplish. After all, you deserve it!

I hope you don't take these practices lightly. Start to incorporate a few at a time, rewarding yourself as you build up to all fifteen. I guarantee, if you will put all, or even some into your life, you will be amazed how it can, and will, change it.

What kind of a person do you want to become? That may sound like a silly question and there's truth in the fact that some thrive on the doom and gloom, and the attention they receive by always having challenges or being in situations that make them needy. They haven't learned yet what it feels like to clear the clutter.

I have learned, to protect myself I need to learn to catch and release. By that, I mean, it's okay to love and leave others. You can show them kindness, empathy, and be an example by being your own mirror. Reflect to others your light. Be willing to share your light.

Keep other's drama out of your space. The World their living in is their reality, not yours. You, and only you, are responsible for your reactions, and you have a choice in everything you do. Don't let others define who you are. Being an empath, I've been sucked in many times and it has really drained my energy and productivity over the years. It took me a long time to learn this lesson. So, catch and release quickly.

This topic reminds me of the time I owned a spa and salon. My client would have a scheduled appointment and a sales rep or someone for a visit would walk in, and all of a sudden, all my attention went to them. They had no appointment, and they were not paying for my time at that moment. Why did I give them attention and energy? You could apply the catch and release in this situation. Acknowledge them, ask how you can help, and if it's going to take more than a few seconds, let them know they need to schedule an appointment. You have a VIP already in front of you, and that is where your attention needs to be.

By saying this, two things will happen. They will be upset they're not receiving your attention or they will have more respect for you serving your clients this way. Don't be attached to the outcome.

For many years I have been giving my energy and attention to the wrong people. Figure out who the right people are by getting really clear on who you want to attract. When we speak about our avatar (the perfect client you create and want to attract), spend time contemplating who you want that to be, how you want them to show up in your life, and then be ready to receive who you've created.

I will also add, if you're asking for something from God, a higher power, the universe, or whatever your belief system is, be willing to receive it.

A couple last reminders…

<u>Love one another</u>. Be heart centered and look for the light in others. When you're feeling low, serve someone else, it will always make you feel better.

Have *integrity* in ALL you do. With so much dishonesty in the world, be one who stands out; the person who rises above poor practices in business and in life.

Be the example you want to see in others. Let your light shine, look for the positive in every situation, stand your ground, set your goals, and don't let anyone get in the way of your achievements.

Be kind to others, be kind to yourself.

Say affirmations every day and know you are enough.

Be a peacekeeper. Look for the good in others.

Breathe. Doing this, always reminds me to pause, be present, and to be aware of my surroundings.

If you're looking to shine, surround yourself with light and hang out in positive environments. Remember, light attracts light. Be the light you want to see in life and in others.

Every day is a clean slate to stand up and be your own light. ~Holly Porter

About the Author

Holly Porter is the CEO and Founder of Prosperity Profilers LLC. She leads her clients through their million-dollar profiles, both personal and business. Holly is an International Speaker who inspires business breakthroughs and personal transformations. Holly's interior design success proves her expertise in color analysis, image design, and personality profiling. Holly uses her knowledge to give her clients the tools they need to gain and sustain success.

With over thirty years operating as an entrepreneur and philanthropist, Holly is a certified coach, beauty industry instructor, holistic practitioner, real estate broker, investor, and award-winning international speaker. Holly is all about the relationships with others. Her work with personality profiles and color analysis shows customers their inner beauty, and generates self-confidence. Her unique gift of listening and problem solving is what makes her stand out from many others. Holly states, "Helping clients with personal and business profiles is my passion. I love watching my clients look prosperous, feel prosperous and be prosperous."

Author of ten books; including three #1 International Best Sellers. Holly has inspired and assisted over a hundred and thirty other women, and a few men, in reaching a new level of success; but most importantly, helped them to see what it is they are truly capable of to shine there light to the World, and has aroused within them a new and profound confidence.

When Holly is not working to accomplish prosperous profiles for her clients, she can be found relaxing with family and friends in elite locations from around the globe. Furthermore, you can find her expanding her knowledge through books and conferences, fundraising, and tending to her eight children, seven grandchildren, and husband, Scott Porter. Holly currently resides in St. George, Utah.

Email Holly@HollyPorter.com

702-907-6723

Website http://www.hollyporter.com/

https://www.facebook.com/HOLLYANNPORTER

https://business.facebook.com/YourProsperityProfiler/
https://www.linkedin.com/in/hollyporter

https://twitter.com/HOLLYShaps

http://bit.ly/YourProsperityProfiler-Youtube

https://www.pinterest.com/hollyshaps

https://www.instagram.com/hollys_haps

SECTION FOUR

SUPPORT FOR YOUR JOURNEY

Life is not meant to be a solo journey.
We all need support along the way. Discover how to lean into powerful support that will lift you up. Support that will encourage you in practical and profound ways.

SICK LEAVE

SUPPORT FOR SICK GUY

A Unique Way To Shine
Dr. Mary Ozegovich

Dr. Mary Oz here; 'Therapist, Life Coach and Change Expert' and **I am super excited to share with you how saying four simple, yet powerful statements everyday can 'Radically, Change your life.'** These statements changed my life and the lives of my clients, and even more personally the lives of my two beautiful daughters. I often ask my clients, "Who knew four simple statements repeated over and over again could create so much change, peace and healing? Who knew these four statements could heal you from the inside out?" I'll tell you who knew. Millions and millions of Hawaiian families knew for decades and centuries. **A healing Hawaiian light is now available to shine upon us.**

Let me share a little history about how these powerful statements and healing light have now become available to us. Thanks to four different powerful and loving mentors felt led to share this process and bring it to the world. Millions of people now know about a secret Hawaiian Healing Process called Ho'oponopono that has been around since the 1800's. Traditionally, Ho'oponopono was called upon for family reconciliation and healing and centered around forgiveness. Let me share just a little bit about these leaders committed to bringing this practice to the world, into my life and practice and now to you. Morrnah Nalamaku Simeona, was known as a very powerful Hawaiian healer and peaceful woman. She learned the healing power of Ho'oponopono from her family members, and in the 1970's, Morrnah created several foundations designed to spread the powerful healing power of "Self-Identity Ho'oponopono" to the Western world. Her dream was to help the Western people connect to their Higher Being, in order to decrease division among people and help individuals heal from pain and disease. Morrnah believed and taught that when we say, "I love you, I thank you, Please forgive me and I am sorry," we are inviting Divinity to clean, clear and erase all our thoughts and memories that are preventing us from being healthy, happy and peaceful.

By reciting Ho'oponopono we invite Divinity to heal what we can't heal on our own.

By saying the phrases, Morrnah helped others heal as they released patterns in their subconscious, which allowed more harmony, peace and balance in their outer world. On February 11th, 1992 at age seventy-nine, Morrnah Simeona who was honored as a Living Treasure of Hawaii quietly passed away, leaving the world a cleaner, clearer and more peaceful place.

She taught countless people to say daily, "I love you, I thank you, please forgive me and I am sorry." Morrnah Simeona knew first-hand about the healing power of four simple yet powerful sentences and was willing to shine for others healing and peace!

Here are the powerful sentences that can change your life:

I love you
I thank you
Please forgive me
I am sorry

Dr. Hew Len is well known for being a psychologist in a Hawaiian Institution that healed a ward of criminally insane male patients who had committed crimes like rape, murder and drug use. If that's not impressive enough for you, the unbelievable story continues as he never met with, medicated or treated his patients. His daily work consisted of cleaning, clearing and erasing his own negative, thoughts, feelings and connections that existed in him. He simply repeated "I love you, I am sorry, please forgive me and thank you." He miraculously helped his patients heal by simply saying these four statements. In his own words he would say, "I took 100 percent responsibility for myself to be clean on the stuff in me that caused me problems as a staff psychologist."

In 2007, Dr. Joe Vitale co-authored a book with Dr. Hew Len entitled, "Zero Limits: The Secret Hawaiian System for Wealth, Health, and Peace & More." Dr. Joe Vitale is a Bestselling Author of way too many books to mention, and who also helped bring the healing power of Ho'oponopono to the world. Since the writing of his second book, "At Zero: The Quest for Miracles through Ho'oponopono," it is believed that over five million people have taken an interest in learning everything they can about the healing power of Ho'oponopono. Both of Dr. Joe's books teach that we can instantly erase years and years of negative unconscious programming, which brings, us closer to a state of Zero. 'According to Dr. Joe, Zero is a place of zero limitations, where only inspiration resides, and we are one with Divinity.' Dr. Joe teaches when we say, "I am sorry" we are asking Divinity for forgiveness from within. When we say "I thank you" we are expressing gratitude to Divinity. When we say "I love you" we are opening the doors for love to flow and when we say "please forgive me" we are acknowledging to Divinity that something went wrong and we want help healing whatever is not right. Dr. Joe learned firsthand from Dr. Hew Len all about the healing power of four simple yet powerful sentences!

I am one of Dr. Joe's readers who was touched and immediately felt inspired to Ho'oponopono every day. I immediately noticed powerful results in my life. I attracted a $10,800.00 college grant for my daughter and feeling more protected and inspired. I watched as the more I said the 4 statements the more my daughter's lives improved. After teaching 'Ho'oponopono' to my children and 'Ho'oponoponoing' as a family my adult daughters were inspired to build a family business together. In my opinion, Ho'oponopono Healing has Radically Changed my closeness and opportunities for my-self and my family!

Based on the results I received I decided to host a three-hour Ho'oponopono workshop. The results from the workshop were amazing, astonishing and mind blowing. The day after the workshop several of the attendees called to say they felt incredibly peaceful. One woman stated she felt less physical pain and another woman reconnected with God for the first time in six years. With each workshop the results were amazing so we developed a 90-day and 6-month coaching program teaching others how to Ho'oponopono and get Radical Change within 30 Days. **I have even launched a powerful international radio show called Radical Change Now that is released on several networks and is leading to some television opportunities.** These programs and platforms allow me to on a weekly basis support people around the world to have radical and powerful change in their life. **This is part of how I'm called to make the world a better place.** Fast forward several years later and Ho'oponopono has brought me several amazing blessings, miracles and lots of Radical Change!

After teaching many students how to 'Ho'oponopono' my two adult children decided to take the courses; even though they are very different, they both fell in love with this process and how it made them feel. It wasn't long before I saw the amazing effects the healing of Ho'oponopono can have on families. **Although we already were a peaceful and loving family, I watched as the more my daughters committed to the four statements, the closer we all grew and minor frustrations began to melt away.**

This past May 2017, my children and I decided to join as a team and bring Ho'oponopono as a Family to the world. What a beautiful blessing to have both my children share in changing the lives of others by asking them to clean, clear and erase, in order to heal themselves, others and the world. What more could a mother ask for? Not to mention the complete joy as I watched my children heal from within and naturally develop a closer relationship to one another. As a Change Expert I have the honor and privilege of sharing Ho'oponopono with my students. Just sharing three stories will testify how powerful Ho'oponopono has been.

Meet Penny who spent most of her life angry, doubting, hurting, bitter, and blaming and not trusting others. After taking our six-month Ho'oponopono Coaching Program, everything changed for her by 'Ho'oponoponoing' daily. She healed from the inside out and now everything has changed for her emotionally.

She's so happy and hopeful these days she works as one of my Ho'oponopono Coaches. You can hear her complete story here in a special radio interview:

https://www.voiceamerica.com/episode/102053/getting-radical-change-with-hooponopono-healing

Meet Suzanne who was suffering from paralyzing anxiety, and after a few coaching sessions and applying our unique Ho'oponopono Tapping Technique, she started to manage her anxiety instead of letting her anxiety manage her. Check out her full story here in this special interview: https://www.voiceamerica.com/episode/102176/resolving-money-and-love-obstacles-with-hooponopono

Ask Chrissy who after the loss of her nineteen-year-old daughter in a tragic car accident, these very four sentences helped her to heal and within twelve months she was able to process her loss so she could come back to the land of the living and help her younger two children process their loss. These four statements helped her reconnect with her daughter spiritually, which allowed her to accept her pain and loss. I believe you will agree with me that these are results you don't hear often when a parent loses a child. Hear her story in her own words in this special interview: https://www.voiceamerica.com/episode/102315/hooponopono-helps-heal-a-devastating-loss-and-brings-protection

The same light and opportunity have now been passed on to you. Are you ready to heal from the inside out and take 100 percent responsibility for your life as you help yourself, your family and even the world heal?

Come join us in helping ourselves, our families and our world heal. It will awe you, amaze you and you, too, will want to pass on the healing! Come join us in our mission; start saying "I love you, I thank you, please forgive me and I am sorry." It's one simple way to shine for yourself and others. Heal within and then help us heal our hurting world, one heart at a time starting with yours. How did my family and these powerful leaders have such radical change in their life that we are now shinning our gifts out into the world? It was through the light and knowledge about the Healing Results of Ho'oponopono. Now it's your turn to receive radical and powerful change in your life! It all starts by committing to taking a thirty 30 - Day Challenge where you and another commit to saying the four powerful statements repeatedly throughout the day for thirty days straight!

The good news is we are here to support you and are offering you a Free Gift! You have been officially invited to help yourself heal, help others heal and open yourself up to the possibility of radical change within you, in your life your family and your business! You don't have to do this on your own…so, take the next step. Say yes and take the 30-Day Challenge.

(For a free e-book and more information on how to take the same **30-Day Challenge** as Dr. Mary, Penny, Suzanne and Chrissy visit hooponoponohealingresults.com) Choose three other people you are willing to share these four powerful healing statements with. They can be people you know, you love, you are comfortable with, or people you think need healing and radical change. It doesn't matter, just do two things! Commit right now to taking **'The 30-Day Life Changing Challenge'** and share it with three people. Spread the love, the gratefulness, the forgiveness and the reconciliation.

Now you know:
I love you
I thank you
Please forgive me
I am sorry
Happy Ho'oponopoing

About the Author

Dr. Mary Oz has been a therapist for thirty years, a Results Oriented Coach for fifteen years and now is known as a Radical Change Expert. Her passion is helping others create the necessary, meaningful and life lasting change they want and deserve. The real joy comes when Dr. Mary Oz can help others create Radical Change, Radical Healing and Radical Transformation quickly. Through the years Dr. Mary Oz has studied and coached with only the best; which includes Anthony Robbins, Dr. Joe Vitale, Christy Whitman and Lisa Sasevich!

After years of studying their success and most powerful tools, Dr. Mary Oz has the privilege of creating her own program called Radical Change Now. In the past four years, she has been honored and privileged to watch her clients grow beyond their own requests, while also falling more in love with their lives. Even more exciting is when her clients uncover their true worth and value and build a bigger, better, brighter future than they ever believed or imagined!

If you are ready for more love, more money, more peace and inspiration! If you are ready to discover your true worth and commit to Radical Change, Radical Healing and Radical Transformation by setting a Healing Foundation in your life with Ho'oponopono, the Law of Attraction and Results Oriented Living we are here and ready to help. You can check out Dr. Mary Oz on her Voice America Talk Radio show called Radical Change Now at the link below:

https://www.voiceamerica.com/show/2691/radical-change-now

Email Address - drmaryoz7@gmail.com

Phone number – 1 833 447 CHANGE

Websites

https://radicalchangenow.com

hooponoponohealingresults.com

http://drmaryozfreegifts.com

Social Media Links

https://www.facebook.com/drmaryoz/

https://twitter.com/drmaryoz7

https://www.instagram.com/dr.maryoz/

Three Steps - To End The Overwhelm!
Mary Shores

If you are anything like me, you have had periods in your life that were so full of *overwhelming chaos* and tragedy that you honestly didn't know if you would ever be able to fully recover. Do these times sound familiar? Times when you passed every day feeling blue or sad and eventually graduated to suffocating, full-blown depression—the kind that left you empty and hurting all at the same time. It's awful right? I know how you feel. I've been there. I was there just last year.

It was winter and I knew I probably had seasonal depression, but something felt different. I felt overwhelmed with life and I had no energy. I was just depleted in every single way. A few weeks went by and I just felt worse and worse. I was scared this was becoming a serious problem, and it was really beginning to affect my work.

What I've noticed (and maybe you have too) is that during these episodes of my life, I tend to have very similar habits. One of those habits that always seem to pop up when I feel the absolute worst is procrastination. I would feel so focused on being overwhelmed that I was completely stuck and would simply do nothing. Having insurmountable problems can quickly overwhelm you and there's plenty of research to explain why stress causes us to "freeze" and avoid taking action.

It's been found that there are two different kinds of procrastinators: Chronic procrastinators and situational procrastinators. Most people are *situational procrastinators*, who will only put off a task that seems particularly difficult or overwhelming. That kind of procrastination rarely causes substantial damage to everyday productivity. The other kind, however, is much worse. *Chronic procrastinators* push off every task, even small ones, and routinely wait until the very last moment to submit a finished assignment and this results in a poor work quality, missed deadlines, and a ton of stress; people who are depressed or in a hole mentally or emotionally, are typically chronic procrastinators. That's what I was. I put absolutely everything off until I was drowning in unfinished work. That's the killer procrastination cycle. Stress leads to avoiding work which leads to more work piling up. Of course, this just repeats itself because drowning in work is one of the most stressful environments for the average person. Eventually, you just freeze.

I froze for quite some time in my last period of feeling depressed. **But this cycle finally became too much, and I decided I needed to do something about it. I went through this three-step process of listing and planning to overcome my feelings of guilt, overwhelm, and depression.** And it really worked. In fact, each step, from naming your problems to making a plan, is scientifically proven to work, and I'll show you the research.

Here's how you can create a workable solution customized to your personal situation.

Step 1: The Problem List

This procrastination and depression cycle went on for weeks, getting worse every day. Finally, I realized that this dark, scary experience must be full-blown depression. I had to do something about it. I'm a huge list person, so I decided the first step to take was to make a list. I labeled everything that was making me feel overwhelmed, stressed, and upset.

Like a switch had been clicked, I began to feel a change. It felt like a miracle to me. I was in a deep dark hole of depression, but writing this list felt like someone had thrown down a flashlight. I could see. This was such an easy step for me to take but it was so incredibly powerful.

This incredible effect is backed by science, too. Matthew Lieberman, a professor at UCLA, conducted a study which found that the act of labeling negative emotions decreased participants' negative response. Putting a name to the feelings and problems really makes a difference. Even just a few words about your issue, activates the prefrontal cortex to reduce the dark emotions while also stimulating the problem-solving area of your brain.

When you've labeled out all these problems, you can also take a moment to forgive yourself. When I looked at my list, I was shocked at how many things I wrote down. The paper was absolutely covered in all the problems I felt plagued by, and as shocking as it was, it made me feel better.

One of the issues I had written down was a huge, unexpected expense, way more than I could afford. I was devastated about it. And as if the dominoes were lined up perfectly, at the exact time of my unexpected expense, I also lost a significant amount of money on a failed investment. And these were just two of the items on my long list.

Looking at everything laid out, I realized that my feelings were totally justified.

[1] Eric Jaffe, "Why Wait? The Science Behind Procrastination," https://www.psychologicalscience.org/observer/why-wait-the-science-behind-procrastination

[2] Derek Thompson, "The Procrastination Doom Loop – and How to Break It", https://www.theatlantic.com/business/archive/2014/08/the-procrastination-loop-and-how-to-break-it/379142/#Footnote

Looking at everything laid out, I realized that my feelings were totally justified. Anyone would feel overwhelmed and depressed if they had these issues.

This revelation was a major turning point for me. Forgiving yourself will lead to some self-compassion, which will allow you to comfort yourself. By writing down this list and accepting that full depth of it, I was promoting a positive state of mind.

There's a neurological link between love and compassion, so by giving myself some compassion, I was bringing up all sorts of warm, loving feelings. Writing the list increases dopamine and serotonin (the feel-good hormones), and forgiving yourself adds oxytocin and vasopressin (the love hormones) on top of that. This stimulates the brain's motivation and reward circuits, which is so effective for reducing stress and improving overall health.

So, write that list of every single problem and realize that your feelings are totally justified. Forgive yourself for struggling so that you can move on. And then dive into step two.

Step 2: Separate Fact From Fiction

So, I had a flashlight in the deep, dark hole. I was able to look around and see which problems were actually real, so removing the imagined problems was my next step. I crossed out each item on the list that was not an actual, present issue or troublesome event. It surprised me how many items on the list were perceived threats and worries. Here a real-life example: In the events list I wrote that a long-term employee resigned, and I crossed out the fear that I had of more employees leaving.

This simple act of identifying which problems were fact cut my list in half (and I could breathe a sigh of relief.) I could see how much my worry and despair had been feeding my depression.

I catastrophized events, which just doubled everything. I could now emotionally process these events and identify which items needed action. This gave me a list I could really tackle and brought my larger-than-life problems back down to earth.

Cutting out the emotions and worries really helped my state of mind. Earlier, when I had seen the long list, I had been comforted in the fact that anyone would struggle with it. But I was also incredibly overwhelmed. I had so many problems, how could I even think about fixing them all? **Stripping the list down to the real problems was extremely comforting and made me realized I really wasn't drowning as much as I thought I was.**

This act fires up the problem-solving areas of your brain, because when you give your brain a real problem (and not a feeling), it gets right to work trying to solve it.

[3] Matthew Lieberman, "Putting Feelings Into Words," http://www.scn.ucla.edu/pdf/AL(2007).pdf

In fact, if your brain is too overloaded with problems, it'll stall. PhD candidate at UNSW Australia, Greg Ashman, writes that "The limit on the number of items that we can remember over a short period of time is effectively a limit on our processing power…" and that if we want to solve these problems, it limits our processing power even further.

Simplifying these issues and identifying which ones are real can-do wonders for our mental state. You'll feel less overwhelmed and more mentally present, which will help you fight off that chronic procrastination I mentioned before. When I did this step, it felt like someone a thrown a rope ladder into my deep dark hole; which leads us to step three.

Step 3: Make an Action Plan

I had my flashlight, I had a rope, but I was still in the deep, dark hole of depression. I still felt unsure of how to begin to fix the list of problems. If you still feel like this by step three, don't worry. Even with the list being cut down, it's still easy to see all these problems and falter.

The final step is to create an action plan so you can start making moves to pull yourself out of the hole. For each problem and event, I had, I began to come up with solutions. Once I had the end result in mind, I followed all of the steps for my One-Page Action plan. I thought of my end goal, and I came up with six things that needed to be true to accomplish that goal. Then I broke each of those down into three more steps to take.

So, for the long-time employee leaving, I realized I needed to hire a replacement. I broke that down into six steps, one of which was to post the job opening on sites like LinkedIn. Within that step of posting the job opening, I included three smaller tasks like writing the job description and more.

So now, rather than all these issues, I had solutions. Even better, I had small, doable steps I could easily take to accomplish that goal and fix the problem. It was like finally heaving my-self out of the hole and taking a deep breath of fresh air.

Taking action can often be the scariest part; researchers have discovered what they call activation energy. This is exactly what it sounds like: it takes more energy to start a project than it does to keep it going. **Once you have something in motion, it's easier to stay in motion.** The action of creating a plan and breaking the task into smaller steps means that each step will require less activation energy

[4] Greg Ashman, "Understand Your Brain to Help Solve Problems," https://www.weforum.org/agenda/2015/11/understand-your-brain-to-help-solve-problems/

[5]Jamie L. Kurtz, Ph.D., "Activation Energy: How it Keeps Happiness at a Distance," https://www.psychologytoday.com/blog/happy-trails/201607/activation-energy-how-it-keeps-happiness-distance.

So, if you split it into baby steps, you can take those steps much easier. It keeps getting better and better because the more you get done and each time you check something off your list the reward centers of your brain are stimulated and the more hits of happiness you get.

So, write down what has to be done, and just take that tiny first step to get started.

You're probably thinking, there's no way it can be this simple and I assure you that it is. Will you still encounter sadness and dark times; 'Definitely.' This is real life. But now you have a solid plan to help you climb out of the hole you sometimes find yourself in.

All you have to do is follow these three steps:

1. Make a problem list and forgive yourself
2. Separate fact from fiction

3. Make a plan and take action.

   Depression, sadness and overwhelm are normal from time to time, and of course you will experience them again. But you can take steps to fight them, come back to center, and you can be happy again.

   By building this practice into your life you will be able to consistently move through overwhelm powerfully and purposefully, so that you can keep stepping forward in your life, business, and purpose.

   If you would like additional support and ideas we would love to share with you. Subscribe to my weekly newsletter for insider tips, free worksheets, and special announcements. Find the info to join, as well as free gifts and access to my exclusive Fearless Ambition Facebook group on my website, maryshores.com. I wish you great success in moving through the over whelm; so you can step forward and SHINE!

   Massive love, ~Mary

About the Author

Mary Shores spends her career as an author, speaker, and entrepreneur, generating positive and pragmatic solutions for people who are freaking out. Mary blends personal experience with her extensive knowledge of neuroscience and human behavior to guide businesses and individuals to defeat the freak out and create their ideal life.

https://twitter.com/mary_shores
https://www.instagram.com/mary_shores/
https://www.facebook.com/shoresmary/

The Truth about Hormones
Dr. Liz Lyster, MD, MPH

It is your birthright to have the second half of your life be as magical as the first. Instead, what I see all too often are women hitting midlife with frustration and a sense of their bodies betraying them.

When we are young we take our bodies for granted because things mostly work as we expect. But as we get older, our hormone levels go down, and many of us feel the related symptoms: fatigue, irritability, lower sex drive, less motivation, sleep problems, depression or anxiety.

If you are a woman of any age having symptoms of hormonal imbalance, I hope you feel better after reading this chapter, enough to feel good about using the right kinds of hormone therapy to relieve your symptoms and help you get back to living your life to its fullest.

If you are suffering because you are afraid of using hormone therapy to feel better, then this chapter aims to remove this fear and empower you and your body.

Menopause is a natural life transition. However, if it brings on these symptoms, most doctors will treat these symptoms with drugs, such as sleeping pills and anti-depressants.

Instead, what if you could address the root cause, clear up these symptoms, and feel like yourself again with safe and natural ways of restoring hormone levels?

I have good news: **You can!**

As an OB/GYN doctor, I am passionate about helping women not only to *not suffer* but to actually *feel awesome* in midlife and beyond. My first step is helping women understand that the right kind of hormone therapy can be safe and effective. Instead of being afraid of hormone replacement therapy, it can help you fulfill your goals and dreams.

Why talk about hormone therapy now?

Around the year 1800, only about 5% of women reached age fifty. By 1900, about half of women reached age fifty. Today, about half of women at age fifty can expect to live into their eighties and beyond. Living so much longer is an amazing modern problem!

My story

I went into menopause when I was 43 years young. What a shock and surprise!

My period had been acting up for a few years, but I found out for sure through simple blood work I ran on myself when I was writing my first book.

Raised by a strong mom, who is also a doctor, I have never been one to tolerate not feeling great. My mom, like many women of her generation, had a hysterectomy in her 30's, so I didn't know what to expect for myself regarding menopause. As a doctor, I became committed to helping women avoid major surgery and address their health issues as naturally as possible.

In fact, my passion to help other women feel great borders on impatience when I see women delay getting help!

Because I knew the science, I was not afraid of hormones. As soon as my first hot flash hit, I reached into the sample closet in my office and put on an estrogen patch. I started feeling better within hours.

You don't have to be as 'gung-ho' about hormone therapy as I am. But I do invite you to **reject the idea of 'just'** as in, "you're **just** getting older; therefore, you have to **just** accept feeling [fill in the blank]: overheated, fat, tired, cranky, or weak."

Even if you are already using hormone therapy, you might still feel a nagging concern about its safety. If this is you, you're going to feel so much better after you read this chapter!

Let's clear up some terminology:

Menopause

Natural menopause starts when a woman has gone for one full year without her period. In the United States this happens at an average age of 51. Surgical menopause happens when a woman has her ovaries removed. If a woman has a hysterectomy and still has her ovaries, it's usually hard to pinpoint when she is completely in menopause. We can usually tell by symptoms combined with hormone levels.

Perimenopause

This refers to a span of time up to 10 years (or more) before actual menopause. Changes in your menstrual cycle, mood or sleeping patterns can be due to perimenopause. I like to use this word broadly, because it takes these symptoms out of the medical disease realm (where they are treated with "Band-Aid" drugs) and puts them in the hormone imbalance realm where they belong and can be best treated by fixing the root cause.

Menopausal Transition

This is a one to two-year time frame of irregular periods and increasing classic menopause symptoms, such as hot flashes, night sweats and vaginal dryness. In some women it can last even longer than 2 years before her period finally stops for one whole year and menopause has officially arrived.

Why is there so much fear around hormone therapy?

Nowadays, there are two major areas of fear around hormone replacement therapy (HRT) for women - breast cancer and cardiovascular disease. Here's a little background and history around this fear.

In the 1970's, doctors promoted estrogen as "the fountain of youth". Soon after, they learned they needed to add a progestin to the estrogen to avoid uterine cancer. By the 1990's, the estrogen/progestin combination seemed so promising for women's health that the maker of the most common HRT products joined forces with the National Institutes of Health to set up the Women's Health Initiative (WHI) Study.

In 2002, the WHI published its first findings with some alarming headlines.

The arm of the study with women taking both estrogen and progestin was stopped ahead of schedule, when they found in these women an **increase in breast cancer** and an **increase in cardiovascular events** including heart attack, stroke and blood clots.

This caused such alarm among doctors and the public that women were yanked off their hormones and left to go back to having menopausal symptoms.

"Now We Know" - Why we can stop being afraid

After many years of analyzing the WHI data, here is what we now know about the WHI study and why these findings should not cause fear among women today.

1. In the WHI study, women were in their 60's, on average.

Now we know: Several large studies before and since the WHI have now shown that hormones have the greatest benefit if they are started early in the onset of menopause, usually in their early 50's.

2. In the WHI study, the hormones used were a *synthetic progestin* (Provera®) and *estrogen by mouth* (Premarin®).

Now we know: Again, several large studies, both in the U.S. and Europe before and since the WHI have now shown that the **synthetic progestin Provera® increases the risk of breast cancer**; *bioidentical* **progesterone does not.** "Bioidentical" means it is the same structure as what a woman's body makes.

Now we know: When estrogen is taken by mouth, it goes from the stomach to the liver where it stimulates the making of clotting factors. Again, from several large studies, we now know that *non-oral* estrogen (as a patch or gel or implanted under the skin) **does *not* increase the risk of cardiovascular illnesses**.

3. One more incredible *"Now we know"*:

The second arm of the WHI study included women who had undergone hysterectomies. Most doctors consider that a woman who has had a hysterectomy only needs estrogen in menopause, so these women were only given either the oral estrogen Premarin® or placebo. **The women on estrogen actually had a *LOWER* risk of breast cancer compared to placebo!**

How did this never make the news? It seems that bad news makes better news than good news.

Not surprisingly, the prescribing of HRT to women in menopause plummeted after 2002. Unfortunately, the scientists with the WHI continue publishing papers about the risks of hormone therapy, when what is actually risky is oral estrogen or synthetic progestin. The WHI results simply don't apply to women today because there are so many effective alternatives to oral estrogen and synthetic progestin.

So what hormones *are* good to use in perimenopause and menopause?

Estrogen: Any form of estrogen that is **not by mouth** can safely help: temperature symptoms (hot flashes and night sweats), depression, and low libido. 'Not by mouth' means topical gels or creams, patches, or pellets under the skin.

Progesterone: The crucial point is that you use a **bioidentical** form to help: sleep disturbance, anxiety, menstrual irregularities.

Testosterone: This 'confidence' hormone is a wonderful complement to any HRT program for women, even before menopause. It helps with: metabolism, calm mood, libido, energy.

When should a woman start using hormone therapy?

A woman can start having symptoms of hormonal imbalance long before she stops having her period.

Progesterone levels may start to fall as early as in our thirties, causing sleep and mood problems. In our forties, ovarian production of estrogen changes (up AND down), which combined with less progesterone can make the menstrual period irregular and mood even worse.

Instead of recognizing these problems as hormone-related, conventional doctors usually either treat the symptoms instead of the cause (such as depression, anxiety and sleep disturbance) or use synthetic hormones (such as controlling an irregular cycle with birth control pills).

Many women suffer for years before starting hormone therapy, either because they are afraid of hormones or because their doctor tells them it's not menopause-related if they are still having their period.

I'm on a mission to end this suffering by helping women explore their options. This will help women feel better, stronger, and more balanced.

Here are some frequently asked questions about hormone therapy:

How long can a woman use hormone therapy?

This is the most common question I get.

There is a spectrum of doctors: on one end are conventional doctors and on the other end are anti-aging doctors.

The conventional end of the spectrum says you should only use hormone therapy long enough to address symptoms, and then you should taper down and get completely off of hormones as soon as possible.

On the opposite extreme are anti-aging doctors who think everyone should restore their hormone levels to that of a teenager and stay on hormone therapy forever.

I think the truth falls in between (as usual).

The medical literature supports the long-term use of at least a small amount of estrogen in order to help our bones stay strong. In fact, the amount of estrogen our bones need is not enough to help any of the other symptoms that higher dosing of estrogen is wonderful for (like hot flashes, night sweats, irritability, and vaginal dryness).

I personally plan to use at least a little bit of estrogen forever. Why? Because I don't want a hip fracture! The complication and death rates after hip fracture are much worse than after breast cancer.

Does every woman need to use hormones?

If you live a perfectly stress-free life or you are not suffering from hormone related symptoms such as fatigue, mood or sleep problems, bone loss, or decreased sexual function, then maybe you don't need any hormone supplementation.

But, if you are suffering even a little, and not on hormone therapy out of fear, then suffer no more.

With bioidentical hormone therapy, you can safely and effectively balance your hormones, even restoring them back to the levels you had when you were chronologically younger.

I'm not talking about just *managing* menopause. I am talking about *being* in menopause and feeling great. I want you to be empowered, informed and know the options that are out there to support you in being all that you are called to be, want to be, and feel great while you step forward powerfully in your life.

My Question to you is: How magical do you want the second half of _your_ life to be?

Remember, looking into your health and exploring your options can give you an understanding of where you are now and where you can go. Empowered with this information, you can decide what the next best step is for you to feel great and step forward and SHINE in your body and your life.

Here are five simple steps you can take to see if getting support around your hormones will help you move forward powerfully:

1. Identify your symptoms: Don't let doctors tell you that fatigue, weight gain, or loss of sex drive and motivation are "normal" or that you're "just" getting older.

2. Get your hormones checked: basic hormone tests include estradiol progesterone, testosterone, DHEA-sulfate and Vitamin D.

3. Interpret the lab test results for what is **optimal**, not just in "the normal range".

4. Consider your hormone therapy options, including estrogen through your skin and bioidentical progesterone.

5. Work with health care practitioners who support you as a whole person – who address your hormonal health and wellness, mental well-being, nutrition and spirit.

You can connect with me through my free monthly e-newsletter. By joining my community on my web site www.DrLizMD.com, you'll receive my full report on the Women's Health Initiative study, as well as latest updates for feeling your best at every age.

Managing and supporting your body and hormones will help you live a happy, healthy, vibrant and balanced life.

Remember, it is your birthright to have a magical second half of your life. May you step forward and SHINE!

About the Author

Dr. Liz Lyster, Women's Midlife Health Expert, is passionate about helping women feel like their best selves, so they can bring health and happiness to the world.

Since 1990, Dr. Liz has helped women and men regain energy, reignite their sex drive, clear up hormonal imbalance, and lose hundreds of pounds. She is the author of "Dr. Liz's Easy Guide to Menopause: 5 Simple Steps to Balancing Your Hormones and Feeling Like Yourself Again".

After graduating from Cornell University with honors, Dr. Liz completed medical school at the University of California, Irvine, followed by her OB/GYN residency in Los Angeles. To expand her commitment to teaching, Dr. Liz achieved a Masters of Public Health degree from UCLA in Community Health Education. In addition to her private medical practice, Dr. Liz also currently also teaches at Notre Dame de Namur University in Belmont, California.

Dr. Liz practices what she preaches. To model growing older with grace, agility and power, Dr. Liz celebrated turning 50 by climbing Mt. Kilimanjaro. She is a continuous learner, having logged thousands of hours as a leader, participant, or volunteer in personal development programs since the age of 19. She is a wife, a mother of two sons, and an avid hiker and Argentine tango dancer. She is fluent in Spanish.

Dr. Liz is dedicated to people expanding their idea of optimal health beyond medicine to include nutrition, physical activity, and spirit. You can contact Dr. Liz through her web site at www.DrLizMD.com.

You are invited to join her online community at www.DrLizMD.com and receive free monthly updates on latest health information and inspiration!

Email Address: drliz@drlizmd.com

Phone Number (844) DRLIZMD -

(844) 375-4963

Website - www.DrLizMD.com

Facebook pages @DrLizLyster

Elizabeth Lyster

LinkedIn Page - Dr. Liz Lyster

Twitter handle - drlizlyster

YouTube Channel - Elizabeth Lyster

Instagram: drlizlyster

Pinterest: Doctor Liz Lyster

Money Talks!
Prevent Yours From Saying Good-bye!
Robert & Deanna Goldsmith

Would you get on an airplane if you didn't know where it was going? Of course not! Why then wouldn't you have that same attitude about your money? Most people have no idea where their money is taking them; nevertheless, they continue doing the same things with their money over and over again. *I know… wouldn't it be awesome if our money really could talk, warning us of the evils that lurk?* Well, Yeah! But, that's never gonna happen!

What has happened is that at some point, every one of us has echoed this sentiment: *"If I only knew then what I know now, I would have done (something) differently."* From the person we dated or even married, to the job opportunities we didn't take, or the investments we "coulda, woulda, shoulda, made; there is always one decision, if made differently, could have dramatically changed our lives. It's those times we "zigged" but wish we'd "zagged."

But today is a new day! No more gazing in the rearview mirror feeling sorry for yourself. It's time to put your foot on the gas pedal -- full steam ahead! But this time I want you to move forward with a different set of rules, with the information you wish you had before, and, in an area where most people can *really* use some help…MONEY!

That's Right, M-O-N-E-Y! I find nothing makes a person's physical and emotional life less stressful than having financial security. And, I would like to assist you with that by helping you develop a new "money" aptitude! Allow me to emphasize the difference between the proverbial *haves* and the *have not's* using a real-life story.

A long, long time ago... Well, 1984 --Christmas Time -- Shopping Mall -- Hollywood, Florida

Assuming you're old enough, you may recall the days when people actually had to leave their homes to do their holiday shopping. And, if you remember that, you'll also recall that finding a parking space during the holidays was as difficult as finding the perfect gift for that certain someone.

On this particular day, there was an older lady searching for a place to park for almost fifteen minutes, which seemed like an eternity! When she finally came across a spot, it was one of those that required her to parallel park--you know, where you have to pull forward, then back in. Well, as she began to pull forward, a young man in a little Fiat Spider "zoomed" into that spot from behind her.

As you can imagine, she was ticked. She got out of her car, hands flailing, and yelled at the young man. "How could you do that? You saw me backing into that spot!" And, with a smug, arrogant attitude he shouted "Hey, Lady, that's what you can do when you're young and quick!" Now, she was *really* ticked. But, what I haven't told you was this little old lady; she was driving a Rolls Royce. Then, as the young man started walking away, he heard the sound of metal *crunching*. Turning around, he saw that old lady slamming the back of her Rolls Royce into his sports car! Not once, not twice, but over and over again. As the young man raced back to his car, he screamed, "Stop! You're destroying my car! How can you do that?" To which she responded, "Well, Son, that's what you can do when you're old and rich!"

While this story may be amusing, (and no, I'm not condoning road rage), it emphasizes a few important yet significant facts about life, YOUR life! What facts? Glad you asked. Like it or not, **"Money Is Power!"**

Now, I am not suggesting power in an *evil* sort of way. However, I am suggesting that money is one of the driving forces of our lives. In fact, the legendary Zig Ziglar once said, "Money isn't important, but it ranks right up there with oxygen!"

Some might proclaim, "Money isn't everything, there are more important things in life." **To which I would respond,** *Why choose*? **Why not have both?** For example, why can't you have money and a great spouse, money and great kids, money and a great relationship with God? The Truth is you can, most don't! Many focus only on earning money, and rightfully so, earning money isn't easy. But knowing how to manage, control and keep more of what you earn is equally, if not more important.

Understanding *money* requires more than a high school diploma, a college degree, or "street smarts." It's a specialized knowledge of how *money product*s work. Or more importantly, how each product *can* work, better yet... how they can work best <u>for you</u>! We call that "Financial Intelligence." So, what about you? Do you know your financial IQ?

There are numerous financial literacy exams online. Not surprisingly, most participants fail. Sadly, women tend to fail more often than men in spite of the fact **financial literacy is more important for women**. Here's why: Women are often left out of household financial decisions, even though most women outlive their male counterparts! Some get divorced --a few never marry, ultimately making them responsible for important decisions without the proper information.

Can you believe, some people actually think that government programs such as Medicare, Welfare, or Social Security will take care of them? Let's put that to rest! The government doesn't "really" care! It's my opinion that many government programs are intent on keeping *you in the dark*, because the less you know, the more easily you can be manipulated. I'll bet most of you are not aware that government regulations make it possible to <u>TAX YOU TWICE ON SOCIAL SECURITY</u>!

Why Me?

For three decades, I have been a financial professional. Not the career I dreamed about, but apparently, God's plan for me. Unfortunately, I lost my dad at an early age, and my family had no financial plan. In fact, my dad didn't even own a life insurance policy. My mom was a "stay at home mom," but with less than a high school education, she was limited in what she could provide. The results -- **Devastating!** She was forced to sell our home even though there was only a small monthly mortgage payment.

One day God (apparently working through a co-worker), tapped me on the shoulder and gave me my directions for life. He said, "Robert, your mission, *should you decide to accept it*, is to help other families avoid the financial tragedy yours has suffered. After thirty years, I know I've served well. The key to my success (in an industry where most who try fail) is my ability to seek out and create unique strategies others do not know. Today, I have the privilege to assist and educate you, *and how I do that, may surprise you.*

Now, it's impossible to share everything you'll need to know in one chapter. Therefore, we encourage you to reach out to us for assistance and to <u>get your hands on Robert's tell-all book</u>; "***From Diapers to It Depends***

™." In it, you'll find those concepts and strategies most people are oblivious to (including many advisors), ideas stretching beyond widespread beliefs, and solutions to many different financial circumstances. And, yes, the answers are different for everyone…the reason why the latter portion of the title reads; "*It Depends!*" Because everything you do, every decision you make, every dollar you save or invest, *affects you* and therefore should *depend* on you, your income, your family, your goals and your life's circumstances.

To best assist you, we've created the **Financial Intelligence Test** (F.I.T.). We did this for two reasons; 1) We believe we can shed light on many subjects quickly and 2) We wanted you to be aware of the knowledge required to efficiently manage your money. Ready? Let's discover your Financial IQ?

The Financial 411 - Financial Intelligence Test

1) *Adjustable Rate Home Loans Are Always Bad, Since Interest Rates Rise?*

    a. True   b. False

2) *This Financial Product Can Provide an Income Guaranteed For Your Lifetime?*

    a. 401 (K) b. IRA   c. Annuity   d. Mutual Fund
    e. Municipal Bond

3) *Which Program Typically Deducts Their Fees & Expenses From Your Account Annually?*

    a. Mutual Funds b. Bonds   c. Stocks
    d. Fixed Annuities e. Bank C.D.s

4) *Using Credit to Invest is Always A Bad Idea?*

    a. True   b. False

5) *To Earn Returns Tied To Market Indices, You Must Risk Losing Your Principal When Markets Decline?*

      a. True   b. False

6) *The Best Way To Leave Money To Your Heirs Is...*

      a. CD (cash) b. Real Estate (Free & Clear) c. Life Insurance d. Stocks e. IRA

7) *It is Never Good To Lease Your Car, Since You Will Not Own The Car When The Payments Are Completed?*

      a. True   b. False

8) *Income Withdrawn From Which Source Is Never Taxable During Your Retirement?* *

      a. Social Security   b. IRA   c. 401(K)

      d. Cash Value Life Insurance e. Pensions

9) *Growth inside a 401(k) plan is...*

      1.   Tax-Exempt 2. Tax-Deferred   3. Taxed upon Deposit

      4.   Taxed at Withdrawal

      a. 1 & 2 are correct   b. 2 & 4 are correct

      c. 3 & 4 are correct   d. 1 & 4 are correct

10) *Savings inside this Product Avoids Negative Consequences on A Student's Eligibility for College Financial Aid?*

      a. Coverdells   b. Life Insurance   c. 529 Plans
      d. Stocks   e. Mutual Funds

So, how did you fare? Before searching for the answers... they're not here. They are available on our website: www.Financial411.Net. Simply click on *Step forward & Shine* for the answers.

If you got at least seven right, congratulations, you're ahead of the curve. Although, you may still be surprised by the answers, answers contradicting what you were sure you knew.

I believe Mark Twain said that best when he said:

"It ain't what you don't know that gets you into trouble,

It's what you know for sure that just ain't so!"

At Financial411, we show you how to employ strategies that help you control and keep more of your money. Including, when to use or not to use *Qualified Retirement Plans*? The most *effective* ways to save for college! The best techniques for *receiving your Social Security Benefits* and more.

Financial intelligence is more than how financial products function independently, it's **also** how *results* can improve when two seemingly unrelated products are used in conjunction. It's more than what a product *is* or what it's been **known** to do! It's what a product **can** do!

You can draw interesting parallels with products like soda water, designed for consumption, but ask any flight attendant how often it's used for removing stains. Ask a mechanic how *baking* soda removes corrosion from your car battery? Ever tried rice to repair a water-logged cell phone? Many products can be used beyond their original intent. Financial products are no different. Did you know that one of the most *disliked* products can help you receive more income from your existing retirement plans or create an income that can be *Tax-Free*? Yes, that's INCOME TAX-FREE!

To get you started, we offer you *"Goldsmith-isms,"* affirmations to encourage you to think beyond "that box," to plan properly with your most important dollars, your retirement dollars! Because, as pension plans become extinct and Social Security changes, the burden of financing your retirement is yours! And, outliving your money is the greatest fear of most retirees? Without further ado here's our "Brain Food" to incorporate into your financial life's plans.

'Goldsmith-isms'

Robert and Deanna's thoughts for financial living . . .

- A LITTLE saved today can have a HUGE impact tomorrow.
- Retirement Savings = *YOU today sending money to YOU tomorrow!*
- Retirement has Two Phases -- *Accumulation & Distribution.* They're intertwined, not exclusive!
- It's better to remove Uncle Sam from your Growth & your Income, than to earn a few extra percentage points.
- <u>How</u> you spend money every day affects your current and future lifestyle.
- Taking too much income from the wrong sources during retirement, may cause additional taxes on funds that would've otherwise been Tax-Free!
- Your total account "balance" is less important than its *spendable* balance!
- Taking Social Security incorrectly can cost you thousands you'll never recoup!
- The *right* life insurance can be one of your *greatest* assets... not an expense!
- Control your money, or money will control you.
- Cash flow is King!
- Money may not buy happiness, but it puts you in a better bargaining position!

Got Questions? Call us directly - 1-877-529-6543.

Looking forward to seeing you and your accounts spilling... over the top!

---

[1] *© Copyright 2018 by Robert & Deanna Goldsmith all rights reserved. For entertainment purposes only. Nothing herein should be considered as legal, tax or investment advice. For legal, tax or investment advice, you should seek the assistance of a certified and licensed attorney, tax or investment advisor. *Some of the information provided requires detailed*

explanations. Excerpts from the book "From Diapers to It Depends"™ provided with the permission of Robert A. Goldsmith, author. Zig Ziglar quote reprinted with permission of Cindy Oates at www.Ziglar.com

Robert & Deanna Goldsmith

They say, it takes incredible chemistry to live, love, and work together... exactly what you have with these two lifelong financial professionals. Robert and Deanna Goldsmith have been both business and life partners for more than 25 years. Robert's experience can be traced back to 1978 while Deanna began her career in 1992 administratively before venturing into the planning arena.

Their zest for business and life has been their recipe for success when building their practice and their advisor development program, having mentored over 1800 advisors nationwide. They credit their success to their commitment to integrity, placing the needs of clients above all else. Their business philosophy is simple;

"If you have integrity, nothing else matters, if you don't have integrity, nothing else matters!"

Their story has been documented in Robert's humorous and award-winning books, *"You're Earnings, What You Deserve... And That Sucks!"* -- A 2015 USA Book News Finalist (Best Business Books) and **"BOOM,"** an Amazon Best-Seller anchored by Mark Victor Hansen (Chicken Soup). Robert also appeared on the Television Show *"Success Today"* with Bob "The Bachelor" Guinney airing on affiliates of FOX, CNN and NBC.

Together they host their ground-breaking Financial Talk Radio show aptly named after their upcoming book on financial literacy, *"From Diapers to It Depends!"*™

A sort after motivational/educational speaker, Robert can also be found entertaining audiences as a Stand-up Comic and has successfully married the two personas branded as "TheEnterTrainer."

They have three children, Adam, a Graduate of San Diego State, Samantha who attended UCLA and was crowned Miss Texas International 2013 and Miss International 2014, and Cory a Student-Athlete and Graduate of the University of Texas (Dallas).

Their spare time is often spent volunteering for causes helping those in need, the neglected, and supporting the Police and US Military.

Email: Robert: Financial411@Att.Net

Deanna: FinancialFitness2@Gmail.Com

Phone: 1-877-529-6543

Websites: www.Financial411.Net / www.AdvisorsIntegrity.com / www.TheEntertrainer.Net

Facebook: https://www.facebook.com/robert.goldsmith.9404

https://www.facebook.com/411Financial/

Linked-in: https://www.linkedin.com/in/bobbygoldsmith/

Twitter: @411Financial

The Three Secrets To Business Success Revealed!
Dr. Greg L. Alston

Imagine a time when you become an expert in your field. People all over the world seek your counsel. You are wealthy and live your life on your own terms. You have all the time, money and freedom you desire. You go on the vacations you want to go on. Your children go to the schools you want them to go to. And you have the respect of everyone whose respect you care about.

Now take a minute and write down the three things this expert excels at that you currently don't. After you have written these things down then answer this question, what is keeping you from learning how to do these three things? Write your answer to this question also. Now hold that thought for a minute.

Given your education, training, talents and experiences what would you say are the top three skills you already possess? Write those three skills down on your paper as well. Be as specific as you can.

Finally, make a list of all the things you know how to do that can't be rendered obsolete by some new emerging technology. For example, you may be the best chauffeur in the world but when driverless cars become commonplace will anyone need chauffeurs? The last consideration is to list the things you know how to do that cannot be outsourced to India. Many jobs will either cease to exist or change markedly in the next decade.

The truth is that there are three essential skills that you must master in order to thrive in the future. These are the three secrets to long term business success. You must have the ability to:

1. Create value for your customers.
2. Market that value effectively, and

3. Sustain that value for a long period of time.

There are many trends in the global marketplace that are making your long-term financial planning very difficult. These trends include: globalization creates downward pressure on wages; high speed internet is making formerly successful businesses obsolete overnight; robotics and artificial intelligence devices decrease the need for manufacturing workers; and building retirement wealth at the same time you are raising kids and taking care of elderly parents is difficult.

The world is changing faster than ever. Very few people work at one company their entire career anymore. Few companies can even pretend they will still be in business in 10 years. Pensions don't exist; just savings plans. Social security is predicted to be bankrupt. The typical retiree lives 20-30 years after retirement, and has to make their retirement savings last longer than they expected. Most people have nowhere near enough put aside to last for their entire life expectancy

Essentially the future is volatile, uncertain, complex and ambiguous. So how do you know what to do to achieve success? First you have to have sound financial goals which include the ability to generate income far in to your retirement years. Then it all comes down to learning how to make good choices from a simple menu of three universal options.

You need to ask yourself these key questions, is what I am about to do going to:

1. Bring me closer to my goal?
2. Take me farther from my goal?
3. Or have no impact?

If your choice will bring you closer to your goal, then do it. If the choice will take you farther from your goal then don't do it. And if the choice will have no impact then it really doesn't matter if you make a choice or not. Making good decisions requires the discipline to constantly educate yourself. Additionally, life is not just about the choices you make but also about how you react to the results of your decisions. People who learn the process of becoming successful react with resilience when they have a setback. They figure out how to improve and move closer to their goals. People who don't understand the process react to setbacks with excuses and diminished effort. They typically never achieve their goals. People who act with optimism and resilience will always outperform those who don't.

There was a time in America when kids learned all the skills they needed to be successful before they were fifteen. I grew up with five brothers and two sisters at a time when large families were common and family incomes rarely exceeded $25,000 per year. Because living in a 1200 square foot house with ten people and one bathroom required consistent coordination and cooperation I learned a lot of life lessons before I ever enrolled in school.

One of the earliest lessons I learned was that if you were late for a meal you went hungry. This taught me to be on-time and that whining was fruitless. Because once my pork chop was gone there really wasn't much Mom could do to spontaneously generate a new one.

The second lesson I learned was the tattle-tale little brothers paid dearly for betraying a sibling to the parents. This taught me that teamwork and getting along with others is a much more important skill than being right. It is simply amazing how many ways a little brother can be secretly tortured, when the parents are not looking.

The next lesson I learned was even more significant. When I was five, I didn't feel like everyone understood how much the world revolved around me. Therefore, I packed a lunch and a change of clothes and announced to my father that I was running away. I was certain he would beg me to stay. However, he suggested I was free to leave if I so chose and asked me to send him a postcard with my new address when I got there.

Even with that rude send-off I was sure he would come after me. Yet, no-one did. After an hour of camping in the vacant lot down the street I re-evaluated my family immigration status and returned home without fanfare. This taught me that you better understand your place in the world and be able to provide value to others because they simply won't miss you if you don't. My father reminded me that he had 7 other kids that were equally entitled to his attention and that he could make another one that would look just like me.

What does any of this have to do with making a living and generating wealth? The last two generations of Americans have never learned some of these fundamental life lessons. They have been coddled at home, coddled at school, never played a game that an adult didn't organize, and expect the world to bend to their will. They have not held jobs. They have never been allowed to fail. They have lived with bike helmets, seat belts, rubberized playgrounds, been catered to by multiple sets of parents and grandparents and gone to school on other people's money. They have a skewed notion that all the good things they have in life are some type of birthright. The reality is that their mindset is not conducive to competitive success in the real world. **Here is the powerful third lesson I discovered: If you don't provide value to others in your business you will not get paid.**

If you take the time to learn the three essential skills I mentioned above you will excel at what you do and achieve your dreams

Let us review. **The first essential skill is the ability to create value for your customers.** In order to create value for others you must flip your perspective from looking inward to looking outward. What you feel and how you think is not as important as what your customer feels and thinks. Focusing on what you want will prevent your business from being successful. Focusing on what your customer wants has the potential to be very profitable.

In order for you to have a product or service worth selling your targeted customers must look at your offering and decide to spend some of their hard-earned money on it. Most people only have a limited amount of disposable income. You are asking them to give you some of their money. **Therefore, what you are offering to sell them must be worth more to them than all the other potential uses of that money.** If it is, they will buy your product. If it is not, then they won't. It really is as simple as that. Of course, there is a lot to learn about relative value theory for you to be able to do this effectively but the concept is right.

The second essential skill is the ability to market that value to your potential customers. All businesses need customers to thrive. Strategic marketing is all about building an offer that is so compelling that your customer demands to buy from you.

Many small businesses go broke running ads that never generate more sales than they cost. Savvy business owners create a marketing promotion that is so compelling that when their customers hear the offer they say to themselves, "I would be crazy not to buy this!" The cool thing about a compelling offer is that customers who make that purchase refer you to their friends.

Good marketing is all about building a relationship with someone who will become a lifelong customer. Bad marketers fail to understand the buyer's journey to making a purchase decision.

Here is the buyer's journey to purchasing something:

Think about any major purchase you are about to make. You begin your search by exploring all the options available. You research the types of products that are available and try to educate yourself about which product type would best fit your needs. Once you settle on the type of product you are looking for, you explore the brands and models available within that category of product. After you have narrowed it down to 3-5 choices then you start reading the reviews and looking at the repair history and the overall cost of ownership and finally when you have narrowed it down to 1-2 choices you start shopping for the model you want. You search for the best price and terms. This is a rough outline but I think a pretty decent description of what a normal person does when trying to decide on a major purchase.

When someone is still in the early phase of researching the available options and you try to sell them your option they will be offended and run for the door. They are not ready to buy. They don't even know what they want. And if you have offended them they will never come back.

If you understand the buyer's journey and the types of options a customer is considering you can market them effectively and create tremendous value by helping them figure out which option is truly the best for them.

The third essential skill is the ability to sustain value over a long period of time. Customer needs change. Competitive products and services change. Financial conditions change. Political conditions change. Tax policy changes. **A wise business owner adapts their business to the changing world as these changes occur.**

Owning a business is not easy. But not owning a business and leaving yourself at the mercy of an employer who may not be in business in ten years is not easy either. Over half of all start-up business fail within five years. The fail for one simple reason, they don't understand how to create value for others. They are so busy trying to make a profit that they forget to provide transformational value to their customers. They waste money on advertising when they should be creating an irresistible offer that would compel their customers to pay them to solve their problem for them.

If you can learn to identify an important problem for your customer, and offer a solution that allows them to solve that problem faster or more effectively than they can do on their own, your business will thrive.

About the Author

Dr. Greg L. Alston is an author, educator, pharmacist and serial entrepreneur. Growing up in a family of 8 children, in a house with only one bathroom, taught him the value of learning to get along with others. His father and brothers have all owned and operated their own business, so you might say the entrepreneurial spirit is hard wired in his DNA.

His first business began at the age of 11 with a paper route. And since that time, he has started and sold several different businesses including a Chain of Halloween Shops, a medical billing company, a drug store, a medical supply company, a long-term care company, a property management company and a vacation rental business. He is currently the president and Chief Value Officer (CVO) of GLA Consulting Inc. which is dedicated to teaching people the business skills they need to create and launch their own profitable business.

Greg has been married to his high school sweetheart since 1976. They reside in Savannah, GA. They have two wonderful grown children, Jeff, a Nanoscale Chemistry Professor and Valerie a Performance Psychology Specialist for the military. And they currently have two delightful grandchildren and the world's coolest dog, Gus the Staffordshire 'Bull Terrier.'

Email address: Greg@greglalston.com

Business Phone: 980-272-1695

Website: www.greglalston.com

Facebook: https://www.facebook.com/GregLAlston/

LinkedIn: www.linkedin.com/greglalston

Twitter: https://twitter.com/GregLAlston

Creating A Legacy Through Wellness
Rosie Bank

There is a message that lives deep inside me. I think about this for a portion of every waking hour. I will tell you what it is and I will tell you why I long to share this with you. Perhaps you are meant to hear this or maybe you need to. Or you know someone who can benefit. I think my message is up there with *peace on earth*. Who doesn't resonate with that?

This book has been assembled to encourage you to step forward and shine in all areas of your life. My message is this: ***Do everything you can to create vibrant good health.*** A body that supports you will be your most valuable asset, and your shine will come from deep within your core.

Busy, purpose-driven, success-minded people are smart to treat their bodies and their health as precious gifts.

If you are one of these people, you will recognize yourself right away:

- You want a lot from life.
- You are willing to work hard to influence others.
- Living a life of meaning is part of your narrative.
- You think about things like "playing bigger" and stretching yourself to be distinguished in your field.

And even if you aren't Oprah or Elon Musk, still, your work and your footprint are significant. The words *leaving a legacy* may be in your vocabulary.

I'd like to suggest that there are two subsets of this group of high achievers. I'll call them Group A and Group B.

Group A: Health is a Priority

Members of Group A make time for healthy meals. They keep their weight moderate, they get plenty of restorative sleep, and they avoid processed foods and alcohol in excess. They would no sooner knock themselves out with copious amounts of junky non-nutritive food than they would do drugs or smoke cigarettes. They also have excellent social connections. They have peace and harmony in their lives as these are part of their core values.

This group is blessed. Members will be statistically less likely to encounter lifestyle-induced diseases such as diabetes, stroke, and various forms of cardiovascular complications. They will also be more able to enjoy the financial fruits of their labor. They know (and you might, too) that *it pays to be healthy*.

Another distinction about this group is that they don't abuse food or struggle with debilitating cravings. As a result, they don't struggle with brain fog or have energy crashes in the afternoon; they can do their best work throughout the day. They are creative, productive, and focused. If this is you, then you will know exactly what I mean when I write that you and your body are on the same page.

Group B: Health is less of a Priority

I need some courage here to tell it like it is, because I used to be a member of this group. Please know that this sharing comes from a place of deep caring, love, and my having walked this path. This is the group that I used to be a member of. Heck, I used to be the *president* of this group. Back in my 20s, 30s, and early 40s I was already in the health business providing hands-on body therapy and teaching yoga. However, I was sick and out of control. I abused food and lived a secret life with bulimia. The binging and purging were so devastating to my body that I might be dead by now if I hadn't found a way to make a change. Looking back, it was as if I was standing on a train track, with the Death-by-Lifestyle train barreling toward me. Had I not jumped off that track ... I shudder thinking about how close I was to missing out on what eventually became the best years of my life.

When I look back to these shameful years, I vividly recall how overwhelmed I was by these atrocious habits. Abusing my body with insane amounts of sugary, junky food left me feeling depleted, afraid, and overwrought with stress. This lifestyle is neither academic nor hypothetical to me. It was a brutal reality.

It is ironic thinking about how much yoga I did, but remembering how completely out of balance my life was. Although there was a name to this affliction (bulimia), the consequences extended beyond how I abused food. The layers of self-loathing, fear of success, and a crushing sense of loneliness stood between me and living my best life. Looking back, I see now that having my energy crash on a daily basis, feeling helpless to overcome cravings, and not being able to focus during some of the peak professional and educational opportunities of my life were a great loss. Sure, I have since resolved and gotten beyond these tragic limitations and it took a lot of ongoing work on my-self. But that loss lives in my past and I see now how much I missed out on life.

So now you know why I do what I do, namely to connect with busy people whose lives, businesses, and finances depend on their getting their bodies to work for them rather than against them. Can I relate to them? You bet!

I'd like to say more to you if you can relate to being in Group B. I have a spiritual longing, even a craving in my soul, to show you that there is reason for hope ... even to feel optimistic. This is not a contest, but if I can get my body, my life, and my health on track, so can you. I hauled myself back from the brink of near-death because I could not do the work that was my calling and live the life I dreamed of had I continued to destroy my body. It is to this day the most difficult and significant personal work I have ever done in my life, and by far the most consequential. Everything else in my life that was good hinged on me completing this transformation.

***

The stage has been set. You are reading this if you are ambitious and want to play on the field called life. You are not the "second string" nor are you meant to sit on the bench. John Maxwell, a leadership guru, discovered this powerful truth in his life. In fact, it was Maxwell who, after his near-fatal heart attack, revealed that if he could change something about himself, it would be that he would have done a better job guarding his health when he had it, rather than trying to buy it back after he almost squandered it. He describes his own transformation as *the pain of change*. **Because you already know about hard work, you are a perfect candidate for working hard on yourself. One thing successful people know about is that progress is not always easy, and usually worth it.** We often push forward in our work and with our families. We are used to overcoming challenges. How about with our bodies?

Here are three benchmarks to help you recognize the signs of reliable good health. This is a tricky list, but it is useful to simplify what is a vast topic with many moving parts. In fact, your good health will always be the result of a variety of ways you intervene on your own behalf. It will never be just one thing, or just one practice that defines your state of wellness. (That can be a bonus benchmark – that people who are on top of their health game practice a variety of pro-health disciplines.)

1. Your relationship with food

You use food for nourishment and you have a healthy relationship with food. Because you are a steward of your own health, you simply do not repeatedly put your body at risk with poor health choices. Instead of succumbing to habits such as binge-eating, mindless snacking, over-stuffing yourself, and eating copious amounts of nutrient-void food, you eat food that is healthy for your body. Depending on your dietary preference, this may or may not include meat, poultry, seafood, and dairy. Regardless, you eat your veggies, and do what Michael Pollen writes in his book, *In Defense of Food*, "Eat food, mostly plants." (You also realize that perfection is overrated.)

As business women and men, we need to be as intentional with our health and our food as we are about our business and revenue goals. Pardon my bluntness, but I told you that we need to be honest about this. Successful people who are mindful about their health do not eat food the way an alcoholic drinks alcohol. It is fairly easy for us to equate in our minds how being a practicing alcoholic does not correlate with being an unswerving entrepreneur.

What about food addiction? I learned in my own experience (not in any of the hundreds of books I've read nor the thousands of hours of training I have received in nutrition) the following sobering fact: *If you are addicted to food or if you suffer with an eating disorder, you will still need to figure out how to navigate through eating.* Unlike gambling or alcohol, you cannot go cold turkey with food. You can go cold turkey with sugar and caffeine, but you can't stop eating. This is one of the reasons why this is hard work and why you might consider working with a Health Coach who specializes in this arena. If you resonate with this as an opportunity to improve your life, you are not alone.

2. Have Personal Motivators

Women and men who consistently engage in wellness practices know their reasons for doing this. I call these your Personal Motivators. These reasons are compelling, emotional, urgent, and involve other people. For many of us this is our family and our clients. I work with people who *must* develop self-esteem in order to achieve their personal and professional goals. Their relationship with food needs to be addressed. I met a man at a health fair recently who has a prestigious position at a local junior college. He said to me regarding his body, "I don't even think about it." I asked him if there was any consequence of not thinking about his body. His answer: "I feel like I am falling apart." He had his first coaching session this week. My pre-session Health History form includes this question: *What is the most compelling, significant, personal reason why improving your health is important to you? Why now?* You might want to answer this question for yourself.

In *The One Thing*, Gary Keller endorses boiling down our work and our reasons for why we do what we do to one overarching, compelling purpose with one primary objective or outcome. For example, my one thing regarding staying well is because I love to do sports and have travel adventures. I loved Keller's book, but in this arena, we can have more than one personal motivator for honoring our bodies and guarding our health. Getting sick is the single most costly cause of financial difficulties, according to researchers at Harvard. They even gave it a name: Medical Bankruptcy. I mention this to point out that saving your hard-earned money ought to be up there in your personal motivators for getting and staying well. Thank you, John Maxwell.

3. The mind body connection

You value peace and harmony. You complement hard work with resting, relaxing, finding ways to sooth your body, and ways to refresh your mind. You know it can't all be about work and productivity.

> I learned something that has shaped my health coaching practice. None of my high achieving clients who needed my help to unwind from stress ever said that they wanted to become more spiritual. However, among this same group, each individual described something that sure sounded like *becoming more spiritual* to my trained ear. They said things like, "I learned how to listen to my body." "I feel more connected with myself." "I can tell when it's time to breathe and relax." Please don't get hung up on the word "spiritual", because it means something different to each of us. The point is that when you are connected to creating a healthy body, you know how to take care of *you*, the being living inside of that body.

What now? How will you step forward and shine as an embodied, health conscious person? What does it mean to take your body with you? Here are three practical steps you can take on your journey of creating a healthy, vitality-filled relationship with your body. By extension, your life will be blessed in a variety of meaningful arenas, as I have mentioned throughout this chapter.

4. Remember to use food as nourishment.

Your choices about what to eat and what to avoid have nothing whatsoever to do with dieting. Make it about providing your body quality fuel to help you perform at your best and to feel fantastic.

5. Remember your purpose.

There is a great scene in the epic television drama, *"This is Us,"* when the father, William, visualizes the judge's face to remind himself to abstain from drugs. What thoughts, images, and desires can you use as anchors to inspire you to remain true to making your health a priority?

6. Remember to soothe yourself.

Anything you can do to increase relaxation, create a sense of living comfortably in your body, and connect with yourself on a soul level will positively spill over into the rest of your life.

On a personal note, dear reader, if you do resonate with this and feel compelled to reach out for help, it would be my honor to discuss this with you further. If you send an email to rosie@rosiebank.com with the subject SHINE, I will make it a priority to contact you right away.

Whether you are standing in front of an audience, serving your clients, running a household, or working on an important project, showing up with your body in a state of vitality will inform everything you do. As you look ahead to your dreams and ambitions, remember to look down as well.

Thank your body. Remember, your health matters.

About the Author

Rosie Bank is Board Certified Integrative Nutrition Health Coach and the founder of Health Matters Coaching. She is the author of four books on health, including her newest, *Health Matters*. Rosie is a graduate of the Institute for Integrative Nutrition and is an international speaker, blogger, and the founder of Health Matters podcast. She is certified as a Nutrition and Wellness Consultant through the American Fitness Professional Association and as a Nutrition Advisor through Sanoviv Medical Institute. Rosie's partner in nutrition since 1999 is USANA Health Sciences.

Rosie has been working to help her clients live more successfully in their bodies since the mid-1970s. Rosie teaches her clients to love themselves first. This is what makes her brand unique. She leads her clients to fall in love with food that is good for them and to honor their bodies through good nutrition, refreshing movement, and increasing peace and harmony in their lives. Her commitment is to help others transform their lives through Health Matters Coaching.

Rosie has earned Advanced Communicator Gold through Toastmasters International. She graduated from the Klemmer and Associates Leadership seminar series and is certified through the Arvee Robinson Master Speakers Academy. She is a graduate of the Rolf Institute and the Iyengar Yoga Institute and practiced as an Advanced Certified Rolfer, Rolf Movement Teacher and Iyengar Yoga Instructor for over thirty years.

Rosie loves to do a variety of exercises – swim, bike, hike, kayak, jump on her trampoline, and take long walks with her husband and their beautiful dogs, Dolly and Gus. Rosie enjoys meditation and yoga, veggie gardening, and astonishingly good health and vitality.

Email Address rosie@rosiebank.com

Phone Number 650-740-9500

Websites:

www.GetYourBodyToLoveYouBack.com
www.RosieBank.com
www.HealthMattersBook.com
Face book page
www.Facebook.com/GetYourBodyToLoveYouBack.com
LinkedIn Page https://www.linkedin.com/in/rosiebank/
Twitter handle https://twitter.com/rosiebank

SECTION FIVE

STEP FORWARD!

We need to take action; take steps to bring forward those things that matter most to you. We want to stop getting ready to get ready to someday step forward. Discover the inspiration and actions to take now to help you step forward today!

Shining with The Celestial Spoon
Catherine M. Laub

The Celestial Spoon is my radio podcast and I love the conversations with my guests bringing encouragement, inspiration, and hope. These podcasts began March, 2017 and now appear on 2 networks. Although the name has the word "Celestial" in it, we share with listeners in ways to support and uplift them. It is a joy to share their information with listeners around the world.

This journey began as ordinary then I gradually blossomed into an entrepreneur with different kinds of expertise. On my journey I was challenged by health issues, including a mental illness. I discovered how to connect deeply and spiritually which helped me through these times and now I get to help others connect deeply on a spiritual and soul level. In this chapter I will share a little bit of my story.

The year 2010 brought my journey in a new direction through Spirituality. I stumbled on Angel Communication which became a major focus going forward. My life coach chose 1 angel oracle card each session for additional support and to put things into perspective. After several sessions the curiosity grew and 'peaked my interest' in learning to read the cards. My spirituality was always strong and the belief of angels was never a question. Most of my life there were many celestial happenings as well as seeing spirits.

Immediately after I learned the details of my next steps, and that classes were over on the phone with people from around the world, I signed up!! Health issues were prevalent in my life and at the time the classes began, I was in the hospital. I joined in on part of a call but lost my connection. Then I joined again on the third call where everyone else had some idea of what they were doing. I was put on the spot and asked to "read" the angel card I selected. To my surprise, I managed to do a wonderful "reading!"

My second level of classes brought me a certificate as an Angel Communication Master. While taking these classes the angels' messages began to flow. The first was that of making money doing card readings. Not long after that was another vision of doing these readings professionally in a local store. Half way into the second year, was a third vision, that of my own store with spiritual and religious items to sell and doing readings in the back room. This is a very clear message and I have confidence it will happen in the future. For now my journey took a slight turn.

The next step was working once a month at psychic fairs in local hotels. Most people didn't understand angel communication so my new title was 'psychic'. While working with one of my teachers she shared her belief I could do mediumship. She had me focus on her ill mother and 'listen' and 'look' for messages from her father. While my eyes were closed amazement arose with the vivid details I was able to convey to her. She was very amazed herself, because although she gave messages never really received any for herself.

We worked further to strengthen my abilities and after about a year my added title was that of 'medium'. My talents continue to blossom and grow stronger and I am able to help many more people find peace in the messages conveyed to them.

I began a business thinking this is great and some decent money could be made doing this. But time hasn't come for that yet. My seeds are planted and that time will arrive soon. The next step was to attend networking meetings to meet people and learn how to grow my business.

In the midst of all of this my goal was to write about my divorce from 1992. It was a very difficult time in my life and the stress lasted until 2012. Joining Facebook brought memberships in many groups. In one of those groups was a post about writing a story in someone else's book, a collaborative one. I jumped at the opportunity and this began my writing career. To my surprise I was guided to write something completely different from divorce. This first story is "My Healing Journey" and was very specific about my ailments and how my healing began. I am still a work in progress but am much better than September of 2015. As of the time of writing this, I contributed to 12 collaborative books. I also combined the first 7 stories into my own books: *Journey of Angelic Healing, Stories to Feed Your Soul*.

These Facebook groups taught about interviewing on podcasts to share my stories. I met Tamara Patzer in 2016 and she interviewed me twice. As she is advancing her career, I seem to be following in her footsteps. In 2017 Tami created a book series for all of her shows. She had them transcribed and combined 8 interviews into each book. My interviews are in volume four of Women Innovators: Leaders, Makers and Givers.

At that time the plan was to do a weekly angel radio show for Blog Talk Radio with my angel community. This show never got approved because they couldn't find a co-host for me. Shortly after this Tami asked me if I knew of anyone that would like to be a radio host on her network. My response was yes, I would love to!!

That brings us to The Celestial Spoon, the podcast I shared about at the beginning of my chapter. The first step was learning how to work with a recording program on line and pre-record all of my shows. It was an educational adventure but today talking with my guests and sharing their stories is very rewarding! I developed my own type of interview and my guests love talking with me because they feel like we are just a couple people sharing stories. The difference is that we are sharing their message and how they help others. This is a very powerful program because I created a safe space for people to open up where at times they would shy away from the conversation.

My first broadcast was March 1, 2017 and I interviewed Tamara Patzer, my producer. This is titled: Tami Patzer - Big Message, Big Mission, Women Innovators. She enjoyed speaking with me and said she never opened up like she had with me. This gave me confidence to go forward with many more guests. What I have learned on the journey and when doing interviews is, to just be yourself. Being authentic is what people look for when listening to someone speak. You shine when you speak and share authentically.

I love to share about my guests and am listing many of whom I were interviewed in 2017 so they get the recognition they deserve and give you a little taste of some of the shows. (Plus, this gives you a list of some great experts that can support you on your journey. Remember you are never alone!) I've been honored to interview people from all walks of life, but most are authors and healers, astrologists, tarot readers, weight loss coaches and spiritual people.

I began the show with **Terry Dika Volchoff**, a Transformational Catalyst, then **LaShonda Herring**, The Transformational Goddess. I enjoyed interviewing **Ambika Devi** who is also an author, an astrologer, yogini, artist, musician and creative dreamer. She enhances present relationships along with supporting and counseling people at the end of a relationship. You can trust her to work through your situations with ease with all of her skills.

A great interview with **Dawn C. Meyer** uncovered that she is an empowering coach and energy healer, plus surprisingly, a former Space Shuttle Engineer ("Rocket Scientist.")

Elaine Lopez-Bogard is a Modern-Day Medicine Woman who works with women that are trying to get pregnant and she helps them finally bring their baby into the world.

Trisha Garrett is the owner of BriteLiteTV Channel with her own show – Trisha Garrett Show. She wants viewers to know that You Matter, You're Enough and You are Powerful, just as you are. She is one of my co-authors of Bloom Where you are Planted and Shine and is a transformation life-coach helping people design the life they desire to live.

Another interesting guest was **Jean-Marc Berne**, known as the 'Voice Master,' He is an author, International Public Speaker and Singer-Songwriter. You don't want to miss Jean-Marc singing during our conversation! Jean-Marc is the Voice Over Coach of the animated series The Octonauts.

Licia Berry has a message about women's inherent sacredness, ancestral memory, and relationship with the Earth. She brings a unique science plus spirit approach with her combined backgrounds in education, brain disorders, family systems and being an indigenous medicine keeper.

Andrea Feinberg is a business coach who helps women in business build a profitable, well-run business.

I loved speaking with **Heather Poduska**, an operatic soprano, national speaker and host of the podcast and television show, 'Thrive.' However, her greatest love is helping entrepreneurs express themselves powerfully and authentically.

Jill Hendrickson began her career as a reporter on Capitol Hill and was featured on 'Good Morning, America.' Now she takes women on spiritual writing retreats to Bali, to heal their souls, and write their world-changing books.

Jacob Cooper had a near death experience at the age of 5. He is now a Reiki Master Teacher and has strong spiritual abilities. He is a guest lecturer for New York spiritual centers and Libraries. Jacob is also employed as a Mental Health Counselor. His combined skills help many people in various ways.

Dr. Dawn Karima is an author and speaker, plus winner of many music and artist awards. She hosts a radio show, A Conversation with Dawn Karima.

Kimber Bowers is a Mind-Body Wellness Practitioner, author, speaker, and loves being a mom. She works with Clinical Hypnotherapy, Reiki, Coaching, Qigong, & her personal line of Flower Essences.

Kristina Jacobs is a Publisher, Editor, Author and Healer with her business 'Smash Depression.'

Michelle Evans is a Speaker, Author, Energy Healer & Teacher, Spiritual Mentor, & Transformation Expert. She helps strengthen her client's spiritual gifts and release their limiting beliefs to fully embrace their ability to change the world. Michelle instills confidence on all levels with a loving, gentle, and supportive environment. She does this because she felt different and unloved growing up & she wishes the world would understand the power of love and uniqueness.

Linda Graziano is a bipolar and depression wellness coach. Her own personal experience with bipolar disorder has fueled her passion to support others to overcome self-criticism, handle challenging feelings, and connect to their higher selves. Her clients are empowered to not only avoid the downward spiral and maintain their wellness, but live their best lives.

I also want to highlight **Tracey Battle**; because she helps women 'find their voice among the voices'. After suffering a heart attack, she realized the damage stress, worry & depression can cause; so she took steps to reverse those effects. I do this because much of my journey has to do with healing, both mental and physical. I echo what Tracey is doing because too many of us are affected by depression, anxiety and other stressors along with mental illnesses combined with physical disorders.

My illnesses are many, and I have both mental and physical ailments. I worked hard to overcome, but I have done so and want to shout on the highest mountain that you can overcome too!!

I want you to remember you are not alone and to let others pour into you, support you, encourage you, and help you along the way. I want to encourage you to check out my show, The Celestial Spoon and enjoy the episodes that serve and support you.

Please listen to my interviews to gain insight to my own journey, but most of all, the journey of all my guests on The Celestial Spoon. You can get guidance by so many of the healers, coaches, therapists, Reiki practitioners, etc. They are all wonderful people to work with and to support you.

My personal advice is to make the time for yourself and take as many breaks as needed. When we take care of ourselves, we can shine our light more powerfully. Also reach out to work with other people to support your mission and help you go forward fearlessly and with a positive perspective.

Since I shared several pieces of advice throughout the chapter, I would like to summarize some key tips to help you Step Forward and SHINE:

1. Be authentically who you are
2. Let others support you and on your journey
3. Remember to take time for yourself
4. Choose a positive attitude
5. You can overcome and SHINE!
6. Step Forward and SHINE!

About the Author

Catherine M Laub, Your Turquoise Angel Guide, is the Host of The Celestial Spoon Radio Show, a Psychic and Spiritual Guide, a 13-time Best-Selling Inspirational Author, and a Speaker regarding depression, anxiety, and health issues. Catherine helps people feel better with her positive outlook and describing overcoming her own deep depression. She is an advocate for mental illness through her campaign "Brighten Your Day with Turquoise." Turquoise, because it is a calming color and helps us think clearly. Her goal is to help others achieve their potential without all the obstacles that get in the way. She's had many health challenges and wants to guide others to understand how to live with illness and be able to have a normal life. She guides others through her spiritual skills to feel invigorated and empowered to go forward in their own struggles.

Catherine also psychically delivers information to people from the spiritual realm, their guides and angels that benefit them greatly with their lives. Catherine is a workshop facilitator and does readings at local events, as well as performing sessions with clients world-wide, via phone and Skype, email and in person.

Her favorite pastimes are jigsaw puzzles and playing bingo with her mother at local bingo halls. She also loves to travel for vacation and business. Overall, she strives to be an inspiration to all and to make the world a better place through her love for others.

Email Address: catherine@catherinemlaub.com

Phone Number: 631-619-2040

Website: www.catherinemlaub.com

https://www.facebook.com/catherine.laub.54

https://www.facebook.com/CatherinesCelestialSpoon

LinkedIn Page: https://www.linkedin.com/in/catherinemlaub

Twitter handle: cathysquests

YouTube Channel:

https://www.youtube.com/channel/UCeWwroCru4uRiZds-FAEVgw

Amazon:

http://www.amazon.com//e/B014M7GZA0

Live in Alignment to Fulfill your Purpose
Naomi Bareket, MBA

In order to live a fulfilled life and manifest abundance, you need to be in alignment with your true self.

As the Director of Marketing at Bareket Design Inc., I was flying to meetings with big companies, such as the company of Warren Buffet, who bought our jewelry for big chains like T.J. Maxx, Shop NBC, and QVC. Instead of feeling excited and successful, something was missing, my soul was numbed. *What value is success when you feel emptiness inside?!*

I started to research about spiritual and self-development studies and learned alternative approaches to help me find my true-self. I had a lot of inner conflicts; I didn't know what I wanted versus what others expected me to want. I felt torn apart and confused. I remember my struggles. On one hand I wanted to embrace giving service through my successful business and make money. On the other hand, I thought that true giving means volunteering, donating, and giving **free** services. My family is very kind; my father knows many languages and often people would take hours of his time to help them translate university articles or write books and he didn't charge them. That is what I've seen growing up. We are so programmed. I still love to give with all my heart but at least I'm not torn apart about having a business too. I was also conflicted about taking charge of my life and letting G-d be in charge. Where is the balance of what I'm choosing to do and what others are choosing for me or G-d is choosing for me? *When you live with a lot of internal mixed messages, you are often stuck mentally and physically. I often felt stressed, fearful, anxious, and mainly numbed emotionally.* I didn't want to get out of bed. I would do things only because others expected me to do them. No passion. No energy.

Through exposure to deep transformative techniques and going ***through a breakthrough, I recognized my own voice, found my own spark, and felt I could live a meaningful life again.*** I released my internal hindrances, limiting beliefs, conflicts and negative emotions. This allowed me to get to know the real-me better, discover my wants, get clarity and congruency with my true self. How exciting it was! I realized how ***these amazing transformative tools uplifted and saved my soul.*** It felt like I became a whole again.

This surge of enlightenment filled my life with a deeper purpose, meaning, and divine mission. Simultaneously, my feelings of fear and not having control, faded away.

Finally, I realized that all my conflicted parts had one thing in common, they all wanted to serve others and give more. Making money while leading a passionate life of purpose, allows me to give even more.

To feel true fulfillment, you must have clarity. Your identity, vision, mission, values, beliefs, behavior/habits, strengths/capability/skills, and environment all should be in congruency. ***Your mind, soul, heart/passion, spirit, body, should be in alignment to maximize your potential. This alignment allows you to light your inner spark, and to live a meaningful life of fulfilling your unique purpose.***

In this chapter, you will be encouraged to:

- Gain a self-awareness of who you really are, why you are here, what life you want to create and inspire others with.
- Learn to be in alignment with your true self without getting distracted by other people's expectations. So, you can achieve ultimate happiness and abundance, and light the world with your inner spark.
- Identify what stops you from manifesting your purpose. Overcome what holds you back from fulfilling your full potential.
- Enforce confidence back into your life.

Why Are We Here?

I remember I was invited for dinner at my friend's house and he asked me, "What do you do?" And I answered, "I'm searching for myself." And he replied, "Don't we all?!"

We all search for meaning, energy, love, and happiness. We also need to be aware of where we are, mentally, physically, emotionally, spiritually.

Like a GPS when you want to reach a target, it asks you where you are now. (Or your current location).

Probing questions help you to reach self-awareness and help you to find your inner desire. Ask yourself:

What are your unique powers and strengths?

What are you really passionate about?

What can you do consistently and persistently?

In what unique way do you help other people in your life?

Often, we might feel helpless and hopeless, but without hope and faith you won't even try. *So, you must have faith and see the light at the end of the tunnel.*

Figure out what holds you back:

Is it our environment? Are We Really Truly Being Ourselves?

We are not sure who we are. We might be confused by our current colleagues, friends, family, and surroundings. They want what they think is best for you but that's their opinion.

When **conflicted**, ask your conflicted voices or conflicted parts:

What higher purpose do they have in common?

Just like I realized that my conflicted parts both had a common higher purpose, they all wanted to give more.

"What if I can't?" When Doubts/Fears Come up.

When I'm invited to give a workshop far away and need to fly far and get out of my comfort zone, I remind myself that I flew to even further places before, and that I overcame more challenging hurdles.

Reaffirm your abilities, your gifts, your Divine you!

You will discover amazing secrets about your powers and resources. That's very exciting, especially when we can be so blind.

Have a list ready of your past achievements. Carry it with you everywhere. Have sticky notes of your list around your home/office to constantly remind you.

Are your Limiting beliefs holding you back?

What you perceive of yourself, you project out to the world.

Your beliefs affect your behavior and therefore your results.

If you want to be rich, but deep inside you believe that rich people are rotten, how likely are you to become rich?

If you want to be promoted at work, but deep inside you believe you don't really deserve it, you don't have a chance.

We call it "limiting" because it is limiting you from fulfilling your full potential.

When beliefs like that arise, check with yourself again what is it that you really want and ask yourself what is the advantage and disadvantage of gaining what you want.

Make sure your advantage list is much stronger than the disadvantage one if you really want it.

For example, the advantage of being rich is that I can give more and help more people.

The disadvantage might be, rich people are not kind.

Contradict it by writing on the advantage part something like: maybe they are, but I'm rich and kind.

What to do when feeling overwhelmed or fearful?

- Remember Philosopher Lao Tzu's saying, "Even a journey of a thousand miles must begin with a single step."
- Have **gratitude**. Every day when I wake up I thank G-d for giving me a new day and for believing in me.
- Adopt the Kabbalists' belief that *every human being was blessed and pre-equipped with resources in order to fulfill his or her unique mission.* That's why you observe someone who sings amazingly, and another person who paints amazingly. Everyone holds inner resources and potential and abilities to manifest his or her unique legacy. When people manifest their talents, it brings joy and light to others. When I hear someone sing beautifully, it warms my heart.
- Know in your heart that this is vitally important because your story of lack or abundance will color your world, for better or worse.
- **Recall good memories**:
- Bring up positive memories and pictures from your past into the present to uplift your spirit, feel good about yourself.

To lift himself up President Obama used to carry in his pocket gifts he received from empowering people.

As mentioned earlier, make an empowering list to trigger your memories of a happy time from the past. Keep it handy, such as in your wallet or handbag, so you can take it out whenever you need an injection of motivation. Then, just remember whatever comes to you and feel good.

One time after I took a test at the university and did very well, I noticed that I was wearing a black sweatshirt. My mind connected this sweatshirt as bringing up success in tests. For years, I would wear this sweatshirt every time I had to take a test. It had become my "lucky" sweatshirt.

- **Modify your Thoughts and Words**

Decide which thoughts to keep and which ones to release—much like a balloon--to the open air.

When a negative thought comes up, ask yourself if this thought serves you, and if it is worth keeping.

Have you ever counted the number of times you put yourself down? No wonder there's a saying "we are our own worst enemies". Who bullies you more, you or others? ***Learn to change your vocabulary and self-talk so that you stop this robotic self-destruction and uplift your spirit instead.*** You won't believe how these minor changes create amazing new realities.

Modify your words and basic conjunctions and prepositions to make a huge change in your mood and productivity. For example: When you say something like, "I always fail", say instead something like, "I <u>failed</u> in the past, <u>but</u> from now on I will succeed", or perceive that "I didn't fail, I <u>learned</u> from it." Or "I learned my lessons and <u>from now on</u> I do better."

Remember:

- You can always begin now--it is never too late.
- Everyone has the resources needed for his/her purpose and journey.
- Don't underestimate others or yourself. Believe in yourself!
- Don't let current circumstances or states of mind define or limit you.

Look at people like Helen Keller who was blind and deaf, and despite challenging circumstances became a well-respected American activist, author and lecturer. People like her ***don't let those challenging circumstances define them.***

When you encounter lack and feel discouraged, remember that this is only a temporary setback.

Your dispirited feelings do not have to be permanent. Refuse to stay in the mindset of lack. Instead, turn your gaze toward the vast possibilities--reach out and imagine what is possible.

What is your response? Are *you* response-able?

Take for example the story of Mandy Harvey, a woman who became deaf at age of 19 singing like an angel on *America's Got Talent*. She said: "One day I fell down the stairs, and I couldn't move, and I thought to myself, 'Is this it? Do I lie here forever?' But I realized in that moment that I had two choices: I could stay there forever or I could make the difficult choice to stand up and to move forward." ***Truly she made the so-called impossible--possible.***

You can do the same. Once you have a clear image of the hero you want to be, you can begin to make changes and become that better version of yourself.

A hero is a person who brings happiness to both, yourself and others, you can achieve fulfillment at every level of your being.

In the process you must have **faith**: As a team of one, with G-d as your coach, you have the support to achieve what you want to achieve and to win what you want to win.

Ultimately Empowerment tips:

Remember even when you perceived you are at the bottom, you can always go up--just like Mandy Harvey did by singing on *America's Got Talent*.

Keep in mind that your beliefs affect your results.

Your inner spark is divinely inspired. King Solomon states: "The human spirit/soul is the candle of G-d" (Proverb 20:27)

Remind yourself how unique you are so you get the positive energy and encouragement to fulfill your potential. Connect yourself to the infinite energy of G-d knowing that He provides you with anything necessary. Everything you need already exists and is available. Keep your spirits up.

With that in mind, I wish for you to live a life of fulfillment, joy, and abundance!!!

About the Author

NAOMI BAREKET, MBA, is a Speaker and dynamic Seminar Leader who uses modern techniques and Kabalistic studies to facilitate women to own their power and take charge of their minds to create emotional freedom. Bareket is the co-creator of NeuroSUCCESSology™ whereby she offers her broad experience in linguistics, Time Line Therapy®, hypnosis, neuro-science, and the field of Neuro Linguistic Programming (NLP) to empower women to create lives of fulfillment. She has been certified by John Maxwell as a Leadership Coach, Teacher, Trainer and Speaker, and she is certified by the American Board of NLP to train and certify others as NLP practitioners and as Masters level NLP practitioners.

Bareket is also the author of *THE DEEP SEE: How to See into your Soul and Find Who You Are and Want to Be*. She loves to combine business with spiritual work. Therefore, she loves to work with entrepreneurs. Naomi believes that when you live in alignment with your true self, you can fulfill your life's purpose and live a meaningful life.

Email Address: naomi@naomibareket.com

Phone Number: 443-248-0014

Website: www.naomibareket.com

Facebook: Naomi Bareket
https://www.facebook.com/successology.Neuro

LinkedIn: Naomi Bareket https://www.linkedin.com/in/naomi-bareket-92b57321

Twitter: @nsuccessgy (https://twitter.com/nsuccessgy)

YouTube: Naomi Bareket
(https://www.youtube.com/channel/UCO3UZ5ekNbfoNptOIrW0G3Q)

Instagram: @neurosuccessology

Choose Freedom Over Fear of Judgment
Kimberly Schehrer, MA

Have you ever looked at your life and wondered how you got there? Several years ago, my Administrative Assistant asked me why I wanted to be invisible. I had been complaining that my business didn't have enough exposure. Yet, actions translated into working hard to be invisible.

One of the reasons I decided I wanted to be in this book was because "step forward and shine" is such a compelling message. **I believe that one can only step forward and shine when you give yourself permission to come out of hiding.** I was in hiding. I wasn't even aware I was doing it. I was hiding from fear of judgment. What would people think of me? <u>To give that much power to others is crazy</u>. I got out of hiding and am following my passion of working with teens and growing the Academy for Independence. I'm excited about it. I'm ready to step forward and shine. How about you? Are you ready to step forward and be seen?

Fear of judgment is what was keeping me playing small and I believe keeps a lot of us playing small.

The solution I found for myself, and the suggestion I have for you to step forward and shine is to let go of the fear of judgment. <u>Choose the freedom to be yourself</u> (quirks and all) over the fear of anyone else judging you.

My freedom began with me saying "yes" to giving myself the freedom to be me; to letting go of fears and stepping into being visible. Saying "yes" to going after my dream of speaking is a great example of not playing small and stepping forward into my life. What is a step you can take to be just a little bit more visible?

I have been quieted a lot in my life. As if what I had to say didn't matter. I was very shy in elementary school. I believe from a soul place that speaking and getting my message out is part of my life purpose. I believe that I have something valuable to say.

I have wanted to speak for about five years. I didn't think I was mentally ready to do it, but I knew I wanted to speak.

Synchronicity stepped in and I just happened to get free tickets to a conference where I received an invitation to speak at an upcoming conference. I said "yes" and although the organizers wanted me to speak on a more business-related topic, I held firm that I would speak about my teen subject matter.

Whether or not the audience was my ideal client, the chances were pretty good someone in the audience had a teen or was perhaps even grandparents of a teen. I stepped in to getting my chance to speak and held firm to the message I am here to share.

Shortly before I was scheduled to do my talk, I attended another conference at which the speaker asked for volunteers from the audience to get coached as a speaker. I eagerly raised my hand. When it was my turn on stage I was nervous. I was shaking and forgot parts of my 30-second elevator speech. Now, I was worried about what would happen later when it was time to give my talk at the upcoming conference.

On the day of my talk I was prepared. I knew this was important to me and what I wanted to say. I went into the bathroom before the speech and looked myself in the eye in the mirror and repeated, "You know this. Be confident. Let the judgments go in and out of you! It's okay. It doesn't mean anything about you." And I had so much fun.

Today, I've decided I don't care what people are saying. Especially when I remember that **judgments don't say anything that is true for you and says more about the other person. Judgments are projections**. I'm going to express my views. I'm going to be on Facebook. I'm going to be out there working with teens and helping them discover and choose to create their own reality to make their dreams come true.

When I think about what I most feared, it was other people's opinion. 'Primarily people that I knew.' In high school, I could fit in almost anywhere because I got along with everyone. But deep down I already was a risk taker and ended up labeled a Rebel. By the time I was in college, I decided that I wanted to study Psychology and realized that to achieve my goal, I had to choose differently. Instead of resisting school, I chose to embrace my education.

I grew up in a family with a strong work ethic where I learned to be self-reliant. However, when you believe that the only person you can rely on is yourself, you won't ask for help, support or encouragement. If you don't ask, you can't receive it and there is no one to help you when you are drowning in overwhelm. My father owned an industrial laundry. One of my first jobs was to detangle the many; many used metal hangers from the dry-cleaning business. I learned patience and tenacity doing that job. Skills I use today in helping teens detangle from their limiting beliefs to gain confidence and to learn to make empowering choices for themselves.

Our fear of being judged stops us from being who are designed to be. Our fear keeps us from stepping forward and shining. It keeps us from sharing our gifts with the world.

Pay attention to your thoughts. We are the ones who are creating our thoughts. Those doubts, fears and what ifs also create our feeling…doubts…worries. And I know that if I make a mistake, I can be very critical. I remind myself of the things that I tell myself that if a best friend came to me and vented about a situation, would I reply with those same messages? No. So why am I saying them to myself?

I grew up with low self-esteem, and a lot of pressure to always achieve. No matter what I had accomplished, the internal message was that nothing I did was going to be good enough.

The legacy I'd like to leave, for my daughters as well as all the teens I work with, is that they are wonderful human beings who are capable of living the life of their dreams. Whatever their vision of what that life looks like, they can make it happen. What is your vision? What is the legacy you would like to create and leave to those that come after you?

Let's dig a little bit more in to the concept of judgment. One way to look at judgment is through the eyes of an observer. This means watching and observing a situation and seeing what is happening. Your version, perspective, of the situation/story is how we justify, conclude, or judge the situation. And the more we rehearse the story, it then becomes a limiting belief because we are stuck in that story and see no other possibilities.

This world judges us all the time. But remember, those judgments say more about that person making the judgment than it truly says about you. **I believe when you know what you stand for, what your values are, it allows you to not align with judgments and align with who you are regardless of what the world says.** Your values are one component for creating the life that you desire.

When we view the choices, we have made as mistakes, we make ourselves wrong. We tell ourselves, "I should have known better." But really, it is us making a judgment. I'm judging myself in a very limited way. We can call them obstacles, challenges, or mistakes; they are all lessons we grow from.

Instead of judging ourselves as wrong, we could choose to extend compassion and grace that we are human. That it's ok. That we can choose differently next time. We don't need to get into self-judgment although this situation didn't have the desired end result. A lesson was learned so we move on. It's not necessary to get into wrongness, just move on and choose to trust yourself. Choose your awareness of your heart.

Too often we let the inner critic lash out about something we didn't do so it's important for us to acknowledge the right things we have done. Our actions will quiet the inner critic for those times when we have done something that took courage and confidence to accomplish. Think about that cartoon of the devil on one shoulder and the angel on the other shoulder. **We have to build up inner kindness. We need to practice gratitude. Build up our acknowledgment muscle in gratitude for the things we have done.** And that is not a selfish thing to do at all. Practice respecting yourself so that others will respect you. That is the ultimate self-care strategy aimed at taming the self-judgment.

Many people have told me that I inspire them. I believe people will take action when they are ready to take action. I'm in my world not paying attention and just doing my thing. I think I'm okay. I'm getting better at being me with my quirkiness, sharing my ideas and beliefs. I'm giving others a judgment free zone so they can be quirky too. I lead by example and that gives them permission to be who they want to be. Perhaps even to take certain risks. I encourage you to share and enjoy your quirkiness too. ☺

Taking risks can lead to freedom. But first you have to choose to take those risks. Some are simple and have little significant impact on your life such as changing toothpaste or getting a new haircut. Others change your whole life path: Getting a divorce, home schooling your children, going after a degree, changing careers, or moving across town/state/country.

Choose Your Perspective

We have these thoughts and we have these feelings and we get caught up in the story. For instance, I might have a fight with someone and my mind starts to collect all this evidence that the story I am telling myself is true. And that story is keeping me stuck and limited to that situation; where if I look at it from another perspective, I can ask whether I need to hold on to that particular evidence which makes my version of the story true.

Working with teens is my mission in life. At the Academy for Independence, I witness them coming in with low self-esteem and questioning whether college was ever in their future. Then through our work together, I see these same teens excelling in honors courses, or choosing a different course of action (a job, or following their passion). The teens develop self-confidence and self-awareness to choose according to their values and passions and not those that this reality says they have to follow. Witnessing them choosing a future beyond what they had dreamed possible for them is true validation that I am doing the work I was put on this earth to do.

If you believe in yourself, if you believe you can do it, you can make things happen. If you don't believe, you don't even see it as a possibility and it's hard to think beyond your limitations. That's why you need support in your life. Support in those who acknowledge you and your accomplishments. I don't think we always receive what people say and respect it as the truth that they see the gifts we share. We just think it's ordinary and anyone can do it because it's simple for us and assume others can do it too.

It is also vitally important that you take the time to acknowledge yourself and savor your accomplishments. You may find that when you give yourself acknowledgement, you no longer need or search for it externally. Being yourself is a contribution you are making to others.

Our freedom starts with saying "yes". If we say no, it limits us to play small. Saying "yes" allows you to go after your dreams.

Here are the steps you can use to step into your freedom:

1. Share your values and your mission
2. Pay attention to your thoughts
3. Be willing to take risks
4. Express gratitude
5. Acknowledge the accomplishments of others and yourself
6. Seek support
7. Practice self-care

I am no longer hiding. I will not be quiet in fear of judgment. I don't want you to be quiet in fear of judgment. I urge you to be who you are and let go of anything else.

Step forward and SHINE! Choose freedom over fear of judgment.

About the Author

Kimberly Schehrer is a Teen Breakthrough Coach and Founder of Academy for Independence. She has a passion for creating next generation leaders. She works closely with teens, who she feels are a misunderstood group actually brimming with potential. Kimberly gives them time-tested, research-based, and cutting-edge skills to help them navigate life's challenges. These lifelong skills build confidence, boost self-esteem, ensure that teens can dream big and, most of all, believe in themselves to make breakthrough choices beyond what they considered possible.

Kimberly has an MA in Counseling Psychology from Santa Clara University. She has over a decade's experience working with parents and teens as a Teen Breakthrough Coach, counselor, and an education consultant at schools, private institutions and within the community in the Silicon Valley and surrounding areas.

Kimberly@AFI4me.com

(831) 239-2788

AFI4me.com

https://www.facebook.com/academyforindependence/

https://www.linkedin.com/in/kimberly-schehrer-ma-75161979/

https://www.youtube.com/watch?v=n7MRyFvlZdw

Step Powerfully
Jaimie Harnagel

Ever since high school, I knew I would one day write a book, but somehow never quite got around to it. Life just got in the way. But in March 2017, as I was struggling with some life challenges, I came across an article written by Stephanie Barton with a quote that really resonated with me:

"You did not come here to struggle, you came here to thrive.

You did not come here to feel worn out, you came here to Shine"

I posted the quote on my mirror and was strongly impacted every time I saw it. So much so that I realized I needed to share it with my Women's Circle. As I continued to come back to these words, it occurred to me…perhaps I am meant to write a chapter in my book to discuss how we are really here to shine.

Then, a couple of weeks later, I had lunch with long-time friend, Moneeka Sawyer, and she mentioned she was collaborating on an anthology called ***"Step Forward and Shine."*** In that moment, I had to smile at the synchronicity.

I told her about my experience and she asked me if I would be interested in the project. I have to admit, a lot of fears welled up at once: I have never written a book, I didn't know if I could find the time, etc.…so I hesitated for a long moment. But then I thought…pay attention, Jaimie. This is a huge sign. The Universe couldn't have been clearer. The next thing I knew, I had an introduction to the person spear-heading this project, Rebecca Hall Gruyter.

When the opportunity came along to be a part of this book, I froze. In that moment, I knew I was making a real choice. I could give in to my fears and say "no" or I could feel the fear and do it anyway. I made a conscious decision to come out of hiding and to shine to the best of my ability.

This past year, I've learned that I need to walk through my fears, so I said, "OK, I'll say yes now and freak out later!"

When Rebecca sent me the project guidelines, I realized that I had heard of "The Purpose Driven Practice," which is the organization that she founded. In fact, it was already on my "to do" list to check out the website! This was my second sign.

Opportunities show up every day. Sometimes we see them, sometimes we don't. Sometimes we say "yes", and sometimes we "let" them slip by.

So, I reminded myself that inaction IS a decision.

I am grateful for this project because it gave me the opportunity to step up to the plate. I needed to take a swing. Maybe I strike out. Maybe I hit a foul ball. Or maybe I hit a home run. The outcome doesn't matter.

What matters is that I showed up in the first place and tried out for the team.

I want to encourage and empower you to say **"Yes"** and step forward into your power. Especially when the Universe sends you opportunities to push through your fears. Here are five steps that have helped me move forward:

1. HAVE COURAGE.

Ask yourself WHY you are hesitating, what are you afraid of? Explore and discover. Sometimes just asking the question can release some of that fear.

What you resist, persists. So, say YES. Lean into the fear. Have you ever seen the movie, "Yes Man" with Jim Carrey? The protagonist has to say "yes" to everything, and as result, he finds himself living a more exciting, more joyful life. We can choose a life of fulfillment simply by embracing "Yes".

My definition of courage is to feel the fear and walk through it.

Fear is an emotion...not a reason for inaction about those things that matter to you. Of course, a certain amount of fear can be good. It can keep you safe, but remember that FEAR is an acronym for False Evidence Appearing Real. Feel the fear and do it anyway.

Often times, fear is not what we think. Take for example, spiders. Many people fear spiders. Big spiders. Little spiders. It doesn't matter. But why? The spider itself is not scary. Maybe we let our imaginations run wild and think of the worst-case scenario. Maybe it is the fear of the unpredictability of the spider. It might jump on you!

But what would happen if instead of running away or stomping on the spider, you changed your perspective and thought, "Hmmmm...the spider is probably scared of me and just looking for an escape. How can I help?" How would you feel if you scooped up the spider in a glass and took it outside? Wouldn't you feel better knowing that you helped the little guy to live out its life as the Universe intended? Do that often enough and you might not feel the fear of spiders again. You would just be able to scoop them up and take them out without a second thought, right? Perhaps you might even feel compassion! Okay, so not all "fears" are as easy to overcome as a spider, but perhaps a little shift in perspective could change your script.

2. COMMIT

Remember, if you are unhappy with your story, you can re-write it! Figure out what you need to do to change it and move forward. YOU alone have the Power. I know it can be tough, but it will be worth it. Don't stay in the "in between" unhappy space. Commit to your job or move on. Commit to your relationship or move on. Commit to your art, your exercise regimen, for example, or move on to what you really want to do and are willing to commit to. Are you moving forward in ways that are important to YOU? This chapter would not have been written if I hadn't committed to it, pushed through the fear, and said yes to stepping into my dream of being a published author.

Commit to being who you want to be and what you want to do.

3. BE IN SERVICE OF OTHERS

One of the most rewarding experiences is to help others, but you might ask, how? There are always barriers: I am too busy, too poor, too overwhelmed, and so on. But really, it doesn't have to take but a minute or two to practice a random act of kindness for someone. We can choose to build this practice of serving others into our lives. This can mean a smile or holding a door open or helping someone with their bags. Serving and lifting up other people reveals the best version of ourselves. It is an active polishing of our souls.

This is a little analogy my amazingly talented friend, Roxanne Vise, shared with me to help people understand that their unique and perfect shininess is just fine:

"If you rub a penny, it will be a little shinier than it was and every subsequent act of polishing makes it shine even more. Like a penny, we start our lives bright and shiny and new. As we go through life, we get a little oxidation and dirt on us. But the act of stepping up rubs off the things we've collected and, lets us shine a little brighter."

Your imperfect shininess is enough. You will continue to shine a little more, every day and in every way.

Earlier this year I was traveling and I was feeling rather disgruntled by the usual travel hassles. As I walked through the airport, I decided right then and there to change my attitude and my experience by smiling at every single person I came across. I looked as many people in the eye as I could and as I passed them, I noticed the different expressions. Some looked surprised, some ignored me and many responded with huge smiles. I'm grateful to have not only lifted their hearts for a moment but, hopefully, inspired them to impact someone else as well. I found that this exercise set the tone for my entire trip. It raised my energetic vibration so high that as a result, I was able to see all the wonderful synchronicities that came my way that weekend. A smile is free and doesn't even require your time. All it requires is the intent to make someone else's day a little brighter. Does this resonate with you? IF so, shine as brightly as YOU can.

4. **LET GO**

I was always an overachiever. Everything I did had to be perfect. At times, I would not start something for fear that it could not live up to the high (and very unreasonable) standards that I held for myself. I have learned that by just letting go of my expectations and taking steps (even if the result is not perfect), is a way to shine.

Let go of what no longer serves you. Purge. Purge relationships. Purge material goods. Purge negative thoughts.

Do at least one thing every day that moves you toward your goals. It doesn't matter if it is big or small, you will feel like you accomplished something meaningful. Make this day count! Be mindful though, of the difference between making things happen for you vs. ALLOWING them to happen. *Try not to push too hard or make a square peg fit in to a round hole. Allow things to be easier.*

Let it go

Let it flow

Let the Universe show up for you.

Once, I was delayed for several hours at an airport and I was thinking, there must be a reason I am stuck here. As I was walking around, I happened upon a gift shop where I was surprised to find bins of tumbled stones. While I was playing with the rocks, a beautiful lady walked up and we started talking about crystals. We had the best time picking out rocks for her niece and nephew. Amazingly enough, it turned out we were waiting for the same flight!

As we were walking back to the gate, I got a little nudge from Spirit to invite her to my Women's Circle. I thought…how crazy am I going to sound, asking a perfect stranger to my home, but I asked anyway. And guess what? She said yes! Finally, the "reason" had presented itself. I just had to be in the right place and the right time in order to connect with her.

I chose to be open to whatever reason might delay me. I chose to listen to that little voice that told me to go for a walk. And I chose to hear the Universe as it nudged me to invite a complete stranger into my life. As a result, I now have an amazing new friend and, for whatever reason, we are meant to be in each other's lives. Complete Magic! Sometimes we cannot always see the bigger picture, but we are always right where we are supposed to be. Just trust the Universe.

5. LIGHT UP!

Remember to do something every day that you are really passionate about. This could be your work or a hobby or whatever really gets you excited. Something where you literally LIGHT UP when you are talking about it. Examples are dancing, singing, or playing golf, anything that brings you joy. **Doing these things that feed your soul allows your joy to come forward and you shine from within.**

Make a list right now!

What makes your heart sing?

What makes you light up?

Schedule a date on your calendar to do it. If you want to learn the piano, but can't go for a lesson this week, perhaps you can at least schedule a lesson. Or you can read online articles about the topic. Or envision where you can put a piano or keyboard in your home. Just take a small step toward your dream. Put that excitement out there to the Universe and draw in what you need, like a moth to a flame.

What is YOUR Vision? What do you want your life to look like?

I have often felt that there is no point in just existing. Truly LIVE. Experience it **now**, don't just go through the motions day in and day out. It doesn't mean you have to scale Mt. Everest or go skydiving today; but do the things that bring you joy, that take your breath away and that exhilarate you as often as possible.

It was hard to step through my fears to realize my dream of being a writer. But as I write, I can lift others, and that in turn lights me up. I want you to step into your dreams and SHINE as well.

As you move forward, remember to step powerfully and let yourself be seen. Never let fear hold you back from what you truly desire.

Find your sparkle.
Step forward.
Step Powerfully,
and SHINE!

About the Author

Jaimie Harnagel is a Certified Reiki Master and has studied Animal Communication and essential oils. She is currently training as a Shamanic Practitioner.

Blending her background in mind, body and spirit, she has experience in many areas of healing with both inner and outer environments. Whether working with Chakras or Feng Shui, crystal healing or beadwork, she takes every action as an opportunity to encourage others to shine.

She has years of experience in retail, sales and customer service as well as owning her own businesses. She enjoys being in nature, beadwork and reading.

Jaimie will be featured in the upcoming books, *"Empowering You, Transforming Lives"*, as well as *"Animal Legacies"* in 2019.

Her mission is to lift and inspire others so that they can share their own beautiful light with the world.

Jaimie lives in Northern California with her husband and two animal friends who rule the roost.

bjharnagel@msn.com

https://www.facebook.com/jaimie.harnagel

Is It Me, or Is It You?
Jacque Opie

Have you ever found yourself blaming somebody else for how you feel, how you have behaved, or how you have responded to something?

Sometimes it can be challenging to acknowledge our own role when something goes wrong in our lives.

Regardless of whether it's with someone we've known forever, or a total stranger.

The moments in life where we are most challenged, are the best moments we are gifted with to step forward and shine.

Every challenge I have been faced with in life has either been met by myself with integrity, or with disdain. What I know in my heart of hearts, is that **when I am faced with any challenge, the only thing I have control over is how I choose to respond.**

What I don't have control over, is what other people do and say, or how they respond to me, and my way of dealing with things.

On reflection of my life, I recognize there are some key areas that have thrown up the biggest challenges for me. These have included relationships, family, business, health and death.

For this chapter, I would like to focus on relationships, as this the area in my life that I have invested the most amounts of time and energy into understanding, and mastering. Specifically, I would like to focus on intimate relationships.

I have now been married for 25 years, and I feel blessed to be in a loving, compassionate and exciting relationship with my husband.

But it has not always been like this. About seven years ago, my husband and I were on the verge of separating. As I'm sure you can imagine, during this time, there was a lot of blaming. I blamed my husband for not showing me enough love, and he blamed me for the financial position we were in.

In a nutshell, I thought that he was the problem, and he thought that I was the problem. When you think about the situation, there is no resolution. Because I wanted him to change, and he wanted me to change; But neither of us were willing to accept it was us who needed to change. Have you ever found yourself in this position? Maybe not in an intimate relationship – it could be with a friend, a colleague, or even a family member.

When I look back now, and assess the situation, it just seems so simple, and almost childish. This experience led me into the work that I do now, which is **helping couples see things from each other's perspectives, and helping them bring more excitement into their relationships.**

I realized, a profound truth through this experience, and through the extensive research and work that I now do in this field. **It is that at any time, either person within a relationship can take the time to look at themselves, and assess how they are contributing towards where they are currently at as a couple.**

During the tough times that my husband and I were having, if either of us had had the courage to take responsibility for our own behavior, and how we were reacting to each other, things would have been much smoother, much earlier.

We would have been able to avoid the arguments, the heartache, and the deterioration of our relationship. I often see this in the work that I do now. **As an outsider, looking in to other people's relationships, it is easy for me to see how people blame each other for where things are at in their relationship.**

And, who is to blame us? **Most people do not have great role models when it comes to how to do relationships.** For me personally, my role models were my parents, who didn't know how to do relationships either. They used alcohol, violence, and verbal abuse to get their message across to each other. I never saw my parents working out their issues respectfully, and I certainly don't remember them ever saying sorry to each other.

What I recognize with many of my clients, is that as adults, we are re-learning how to do intimate relationships. We often recognize that how we are doing things, is not necessarily the best way, but we don't always know what else to do. Until we learn a new way of doing things, we will keep repeating what we know, and what we experienced in our childhood.

At some point, we realize that if we do not change how we show up in our relationships that we may end up with the result that more than 50% of long term couples end up with-and that is separation.

So how do we change this? We need to take responsibility and be proactive with our willingness to work at them. I would love to share with you some of the tips that I share in my book, called Passion Rituals. These tools are the foundation that I now use in my own relationship to future proof it. I believe that relationships take effort every single day, and that the effort put in, pays us back in happiness, love and connection.

I also want to stress that the tips I share are specifically for couples who want to re-connect and who need tweaking to get them to what they want. If you are in an abusive relationship, I strongly suggest getting the help that you need to get yourself safe. You can do this by seeking professional help from a Therapist, speaking to the authorities, and notifying your family or friends.

I hope that these tips help you Step Forward and SHINE in Your Relationships:

1. Accept Responsibility for your part.

Okay, so the first thing is to accept your part in what is not working within your relationship. It is highly unlikely that it is all one sided; even if it's just a small part that you are currently willing to take responsibility for. Just like in a car accident, even the claimant has to accept some responsibility. Make the decision that you are no longer prepared to play the blame game.

2. Speak to Your Partner.

Next is speaking to your partner about what you are not happy about. Make sure you choose your timing well, and that you use non-aggressive language.

Then, ask your partner if there is anything that you are doing that is upsetting them. Once you know these things, you can alleviate them if you feel it's important.

3. Together, establish guidelines.

Then set up some guidelines together within your relationship of what is and what is not acceptable. For example, is it important to you that you don't argue in front of the children? Write down your guidelines and keep them somewhere that you can both refer to them.

4. Look at how much fun you are having.

Next, look at how much fun you are having in your relationship. Are you doing things together to enhance your relationship, or are you caught up in the daily grind? If you are not having fun together and building on your relationship daily in some way, then finding positive things to talk about becomes a challenge.

5. Talk about your conflict style.

And now you are ready to talk about how you respond to each other in conflict situations. Do you normally butt in when your partner is sharing how they feel? Or are you the type to walk away and ignore each other for days on end? Whatever your conflict style, it's important that you talk about it. Then decide on how you can do conflict in a safe way, and in a way that actually gets a resolution, and brings you closer together, as opposed to pulling your apart.

6. Create rituals in your relationship

Now that you know how to do conflict and you have decided on how you want to resolve issues that you have, you can begin to build rituals into your relationship that will keep you having fun, keep you engaged with each other, and build more meaning into your relationship. I have written a book to help my clients with their rituals, and a place to start. The book can be found on my website.

Every conflict within a relationship is an opportunity to step forward and shine, or to create irreparable damage. The choice is absolutely yours. That is where your power sits, remembering that you are the only one who gets to decide how you respond.

I wish you all the very best in your intimate relationship.

Love and light, Jacque

About the Author

Jacque is a sought-after speaker and author, helping people create more meaningful connection and deeper intimacy within their relationship, helping them transform their partnership from being about everyday routine, to being exhilarating, passionate and exciting.

Her work is underpinned by more than 15 years of teaching and studying communication, positive psychology and interpersonal skills, as well as her personal experience in her long-term marriage. She believes that if two people want to make a relationship work, that anything is possible!

She is edgy, exciting, and brings humour and respect to a topic well overdue in being discussed openly and honestly. She has been married for 25 years to her soulmate Craig, and they have two adult sons. They are very happy, but it has not always been like that. They spent years feeling disconnected, which started Jacque on her journey to re-igniting her love life, which she has done with great success! She now brings those years of research, experience, study and personal growth to others for the same success.

Web: www.jacqueopie.com Email: jacqueo@jacqueopie.com

SECTION SIX

CHOOSE TO SHINE!

We all have the ability to SHINE! Gain tips, tools, and insights to help you discover how to share the gift of "You" with those around you. Be willing to share the of gift of "You" with the world… choose to SHINE!

Technology With A Heart
Michelle Calloway

It was dark as the waves crashed down on me. Wave after wave kept coming, relentlessly trying to devour me. I gasped for air as I tried to keep my head above the water. I heard a deep voice yelling in the distance. I looked to my left and barely made out the silhouette of a man. He yelled "GRAB HOLD" as he hoisted the life buoy out to me. It landed twelve inches in front of me. I was overwhelmed with joy! I was going to be rescued!

I tried to lift my arm out of the water to grab hold of the buoy, but I couldn't muster the strength. My arms felt like they were filled with lead. I was so weary from treading water for so long that I had no strength left in me to grab hold of the life-line that was right in front of me. I knew then, that I was going to drown, and I couldn't do anything to stop it.

As I woke up from this dream, **I realized I needed to make some serious changes.** As a business owner, have you ever felt like you were drowning? In an oversaturated sea of digital noise, it's getting harder to stand out from our competitors. Consumer trends shift like the tides, which can leave us weary, as we tread water just to survive. There is a lifeline available, and I'd like to share it with you.

My life took a very abrupt turn when my beloved husband of 15 years passed away after a long-term battle with illness. I was left to raise our two adolescent daughters on my own, not knowing what our future held in store for us. In the span of 6 years following my husband's death, we experienced some really great times, and some incredibly difficult times.

It was during this recovery period that I met my new best friend, (who is now my husband and business partner). Shortly after marrying my new husband, I was "let go" from my graphic design job of nine years due to the financial crisis of 2008. **Life felt like a roller coaster.**

When I lost my job as a graphic designer, I instantly signed myself up for school to learn more relevant design techniques like video and multimedia. It was while I was in school that my friend suggested we start up our own graphic design agency. I had never been in business for myself, but I went along with the idea since she came from a family of business owners. She said she would handle the business side of things while I mainly managed the customers and the design work.

This is where the story gets interesting, and my life has literally never been the same since.

Vision and Purpose

About two months after graduating with my digital media degree, I was introduced to a cutting-edge technology that makes physical objects COME ALIVE with virtual content when they are viewed through a mobile smart device. In this instance, I was shown how an ordinary business card COMES ALIVE with a personal video message. I was BLOWN AWAY!! I couldn't sleep for two whole weeks!! No kidding! My brain was lit up with all sorts of ideas.

When something grabs your attention like that and won't let go, it must mean you are being called to DO something with it. I believe this tech was brought to me for a reason, and that reason is bigger than me. I just needed to show up and do the work. I set out to learn everything that I could about this new technology called augmented reality. Months later a young friend of mine saw that I could make physical objects COME ALIVE with video. She asked me if I could help her create a "Thinking of You" card for her boyfriend, who was deployed overseas. She wanted him to be able to hear her and see her anytime he wanted. I LOVED the idea, and we set out to create it.

Once he received the card, he was very touched at the thought of her sending him a card with her beautiful face on the front of it. But, when he watched her COME ALIVE on the card and started talking to him, it rocked him to his core! He ended up carrying it with him every day because he said it made him feel as if she was right there with him. I saw that this technology could enhance human relationships, even those separated by oceans. I knew I needed to make it accessible and affordable for everyone to experience, no matter the budget. Everyone needs to be able to experience the wonder of this magical technology and powerful authentic connections.

As I contemplated building a scalable technology company, I looked at my husband and said, **"It's not going to be easy, in fact it's going to be very** hard. It's going to require a lot of sacrifice - both time and money. But I believe I've been called to do something good with it. I can't let it die with me; I have to see it through." My husband is an amazing man. He agreed that we should do it together. A new journey begins. I discovered it's important to say yes to your calling and be willing to bring it forward. Face the challenges, remember your calling, say yes and lean in!

Learn From Experts

It's hard to avoid pitfalls if you don't know what they are. I had been trained in digital media design, but I didn't know the first thing about building and growing a technology company. It was time to find a mentor or coach. We were introduced to a kind, knowledgeable, and successful gentleman who was willing to take me under his wing and prepare us for investor financing. Our business model was not a good fit for traditional financing such as a bank loan. We would need investors to risk hundreds of thousands of dollars with us, so there was much to do to prove we would be worth the risk.

We were encouraged to join a startup incubator in Berkeley, CA. It's like a training ground for new entrepreneurs. Being a part of this environment allowed me to flush out my ideas with other founders on a daily basis. I also received quality guidance from investors on the different aspects of business like, revenue model, marketing strategy, competitive advantage, financial forecasting, etc. I often felt like I was drinking from a firehose! **So much NEW information was coming at me, making my brain swell. But, I was determined to see this through. I believed this was my calling.**

Our first marketing strategy was to go out and participate in wedding fairs. We believed brides would love the ability to add a personal video message to their printed wedding invitations. We were right! Our concept resonated with about 70% of the crowd. We also received incredible feedback, which led us to pivot to our current B2B business model which is working very effectively.

I've learned a lot about business and people on this entrepreneurial journey. I've learned that people connect better with what you're doing (in life and in business) if you share a little bit of story with them. I've learned that you'll be more successful (in life and in business) if you show interest in your clients rather than the sale. **People want to know you care.**

Experiential Marketing

Consumers now have instant access to information about your product or service through mobile technology. Digital banner ads are not as effective as they were just a few years ago. Nobody wants to be "sold to" anymore. Consumers are looking to experience you or your business prior to making their buying decisions. **Experiential marketing is a great opportunity for us to really connect with consumers, and positively influence their buying decisions.**

Here are three key principles to build effective, authentic connection with people that will elevate your level of impact and influence quickly, when communicated through modern technology tools.

1. **Connection** – *humans crave human connection. Even though we live in a digital era, we are happier when we are connected with other humans.*

As a business owner, one of the simplest ways for you to connect with your audience is to use more video in your marketing. Video allows us to feel connected even though we are not sharing the same physical space. We can see you, hear you, and read your body language. This forms a connection. When you demonstrate your product or service in action, viewers connect with it.

Augmented reality takes this connection to a whole new level as it bridges the real world with the virtual world. It creates an impactful experience filled with awe and wonder not easily forgotten.

1. **Authenticity** – *we connect better with those that we can relate to.* Nobody is perfect, yet companies try to pretend that they are. If you really want to connect with consumers, let them see the real you. Share stories with them via video or live streaming through social-media.

    Ask some of your favorite customers to do a video testimonial for you. Get on a video conference call with them and ask if it's okay to record their responses. Then ask them specific questions that will get them talking about why they loved you or your service so much. These types of testimonials are so powerful because they allow us to connect with the person sharing their experience.

2. **Build Community** – *we thrive when we feel a sense of belonging.* If you want your satisfied clients to become raving fans, you need to be continuously connecting with them. There are

many ways you can provide your clients with a sense of belonging:

a. Email Campaigns

b. Social Media Groups

c. Birthday/Holiday/Thank You Cards

d. Live Events/Meetups

e. Educational Webinars

f. Phone Calls

g. J/V Partnerships

When you incorporate these core relationship marketing principles into your business strategy, you will elevate your level of impact and influence on consumers. Emerging technologies like video and augmented reality, when combined with relationship marketing principles provide consumers with an impressionable experience that ultimately impacts their buying decisions.

The initiative to use technology to enhance human relationships rather than replace them is called '**Tech With Heart**.' In a digital era, where technology is evolving so rapidly, it is foolish for us to think we can shut it out of our lives entirely. What we can do is focus on using it to promote good for humanity. As business owners we can use it for good to promote quality connection with people, because people are the heart of successful business.

I invite you to join the 'Tech With Heart' initiative at https://techwithheartnetwork.com.

May you have great success in all that you do connect form the heart, authentically and powerfully with your people.

About the Author

Michelle Calloway is a Speaker, Int'l Bestselling Author, and the Founder and CEO of REVEALiO Inc., an augmented reality marketing company. She is driven to success in response to a calling she believes has been placed in her life. Her goal is to make these augmented reality experiences accessible and affordable for everyone, to enhance human relationships, and empower business owners to have more impact, influence, and income.

Michelle combines her expertise in visual communication with the emerging world of augmented reality (AR). This cutting-edge technology overlays virtual content on top of real world objects when they are viewed through a mobile or wearable smart device.

Her vision of **REVEALiO** became clear when she witnessed the powerful heartfelt connection that took place when a deployed U.S. soldier received a REVEALiO greeting card from his girlfriend. When the card 'came alive' with her talking to him on the card; it rocked him to his core. He folded it up and carried it with him every day because it made him feel as if she was right there with him. This powerful human response is what inspired Michelle Calloway to develop and launch REVEALiO – Cards That Come Alive!

Michelle wants to share her inspirational story and teach the power of augmented reality as a marketing tool to entrepreneurs, small business owners, CEOs, Video Professionals, and Publishers. Her heart is to empower small businesses to gain the ultimate competitive advantage by captivating their audiences and influencing their buying decisions.

Email: mcalloway@revealio.com
Phone: 415-870-7894
Personal Website: https://michellecalloway.us
Business Website: https://www.revealio.com
Personal Facebook: https://www.facebook.com/michelle.callowaybowden
Business Facebook: https://business.facebook.com/revealio
LinkedIn: https://www.linkedin.com/in/michelle-calloway-revealio
Twitter: https://twitter.com/Smileyshell69
Instagram: https://www.instagram.com/micalloway
YouTube: https://www.youtube.com/channel/UC4LzcwGHM1IJjmLHGRtnJLA

Create Your Blissful Life
Moneeka Sawyer

In 1967, in Bombay India, a man met a woman. As was the tradition in those days, they had to decide very quickly about whether they were going to get married. So, three weeks after they met they were out to dinner and the man Vishin, said to the woman Vidya, "I am going to America, would you like to come?" A big bright smile lit up Vidya's face and she said "I would love to!"

So, the two of them as newlyweds came to America. **That was the beginning of my parent's life together.** They came here with only $200 in their pockets and a dream to build a better life for the family they wanted to create. My Dad had heard that the golden ticket to wealth in the United States was to buy real estate, so as soon as they could they bought their first house.

They soon had their first child, and with their hearts full of love, hope, and joy, they began to save all of their nickels and dimes so they could buy their first rental property. Mom took her beautiful Indian fabrics and sewed the curtains for her windows and the cushions for her sofa so she could have a beautiful home without spending too much money, and soon they were able to buy their first investment property. They stayed focused on their goals and built a life they loved. They had two more little girls and eighteen years later, through their real estate investing, they paid for the college education of that first tiny little girl at U.C. Berkeley.

They continued to pay for their life, they paid for the college education of their two other girls and today they are retired. They live in a beautiful home on a lake with four bedrooms so all of their girls can come home whenever they want and have a room of their own. **Most importantly they** are living the life they want. After all those years of hard work they can do what they want in their retirement.

*****

When I graduated from college I was really struck by the realization that I was out there on my own. The infrastructure that has supposedly been built for people in retirement was crumbling away around us. I was never going to collect social security that was for sure. Pensions were a thing of the past. **I realized that the only way that I was ever going to be secure in the long-term was if I did it myself.**

Soon after I graduated I got married and my new husband and I bought a starter house. A few years later we were going to buy a nicer house, and at that point I needed to decide if I wanted to keep this house and rent it out or did I want to sell it.

You see, although real estate had really served my parents and myself, I had also seen the level of stress that it had caused my dad - the money issues, dealing with tenants, the amount of time it took him away from his family. I really, *really* did not want that life. I did not want that complication. I did not want that stress. However, I did want the financial security.

I was scared and stressed out about the decision so one night I talked to my dad about it. That night he said something to me that completely changed my life.

He said, "Moneeka, everybody has money issues. Do you want poor people money issues or do you want rich people money issues?"

That was an interesting perspective. It made me stop and think. That night I decided yes, I wanted rich people money issues! I decided to rent out that house. But I was very committed to making sure that I did not have the kind of stress my Dad had. This was going to be a part-time business. This was not my passion, this was just to build my future.

Over the past several years I have developed a streamlined system for myself so that I only spend five to ten hours a month on this business. It basically runs itself. Running this business part-time, I have now built, in twenty years, a multimillion-dollar real estate empire. Because of this part-time business I am able to focus my time and energy on running a business and living a life that I love.

I love it when people ask me about how I built my blissful wealth, because it gives me an opportunity to share with them that it is truly possible for them too. This is what is possible when you really

understand the leverage of real estate, and that is what I want to share with you. I have developed the blissful real estate investor formula to help people do exactly what I have done.

How I am defining bliss? Bliss is that deep sense of joy and contentment and confidence that you can handle anything that comes your way. It is emotional mastery and resilience. I am not saying that money buys happiness. But if you feel safe it is a lot easier to focus on happiness. I believe a key to having a blissful life is having security and having a plan for your life right now as well as for your future. I have created my own blissful life and a formula to help others create their own blissful lives using investing in real estate as a tool.

What is it that you want? You can have anything you want, if you set your mind to it. Do you want to retire in style? Do you want to put your children through college? Do you want to build a secure nest egg for when things go wrong in life? What is it that you want?

The number one block that stops people from achieving their goals and dreams is fear. It is the number one block we all need to step past in order to really step forward and shine in our lives. If you allow yourself to stay in your fear, you will stay where you are and never reach your highest potential. Worse, you'll never have the blissful life you deserve to live.

You might be thinking, Moneeka that sounds great, but real estate is not for me. I don't have the time. I don't have the money. I don't know enough. Real estate is too hard. The market is really inflated right now, I will just wait. All of those objections can be dealt with, and I deal with each of them in my course work. The answers and resources are all there for you, and I can give them to you. But before you can do anything you need to step past your fear.

Warren Buffet, one of the richest men in the world has said, "If you cannot control your emotions, you cannot control your money." It is just a fact. This is why I believe so much in having a plan and strategy to help people step into their blissful life. In the blissful real estate investor formula, you will learn how to manage your emotions, step through your fear, and control your stress so that you can build the future and fortune that you want.

To get started, the first step may surprise you. It is to identify your core values.

Do you know who you are?

I know this sounds rhetorical, but the fact is that most of us don't actually know who we are deep down inside. We run our lives and businesses based on what our coaches, families, and friends tell us we should be doing. We make decisions based on obsolete beliefs we've been clinging to that don't actually serve us anymore.

Before you can build a blissful life you need to know who you truly are. In order to discover that, let's get really clear on your Core Values.

Here is a process that will help you get clear on your Core Values:

Start by writing down ten of your top values like family, feeling financially secure, bliss, adventure, relationships, joy, security, learning, excitement, or personal development. There are hundreds to choose from. If you want some ideas or thought joggers, go to blissfulinvestorbook.com.

Now look at your list of ten and ask yourself, "If I could have just one value, what would it be?" Write down the first answer that comes to your mind.

Next, ask "If I could have just one more, what would it be?"

Repeat this until you come up with your top five values. Now, take a look at your life. How are you making your decisions? One of the things that causes a lot of fear for people is that they feel they are out of control. They may feel they don't make good enough decisions. Much of this has to do with the fact that they are making decisions and taking actions that actually conflict with their core values. The more someone does that, the more conflicted their life becomes, and the more fear they feel.

The first step to moving past your fear is to re-align with who you truly are. To do this, spend some time getting clear on your core values. Understand that you won't necessarily get this exactly right the first time you go through this exercise. Pay attention and adjust your list when you notice it isn't feeling right to you. Eventually, you will have a list that is exactly right, and you'll be able to make decisions and take action that is beautifully aligned with who you truly are.

I invite you to build for your future. Fast forward twenty years from now. Where are you going to be? What is life going to have looked like for you? Did you put your children through college? Did you feel safe when things went wrong? Are you living the retirement you want? What is it going to look like?

Think about how you are going to achieve those things that are important to you. Is it your turn to step forward and shine?

I hope you choose to make bliss a priority for yourself! I'd like to help you step forward towards knowledge, security, bliss, and more with the following tips:

Five Keys to help you step towards your BLISS:

1. Get clarity around your core values
2. Align with your core values
3. Take simple steps towards your bliss every day.
4. Give yourself permission to begin building the wealth you need to feel safe and secure.
5. Take one action per week toward attaining this goal.

I hope you choose to take steps towards your BLISS and SHINE! It truly is your choice!

About the Author

Moneeka Sawyer is often described as one of the most blissful people you will ever meet. But don't confuse her big smile and infectious laugh with naiveté. Her multi-million-dollar real estate empire is just one example of her ability to strategize, organize, and implement big business plans.

She has been investing in Real Estate for over twenty years, so has seen all the different cycles of the market. Through her strategies, she has turned $10,000 into over $2,000,000, working only five-ten hours per MONTH with very little stress.

She lives her dreams and won't let anyone tell her what she can and can't do. Even though she was constantly told she couldn't get in, she graduated from Haas Business School at U.C.Berkeley, one of the top three colleges in the nation and has been in business for herself ever since. While building her multi-million-dollar business, she has travelled to over fifty-five countries, dances every single day, and spends lots of time with her husband of over twenty years and her adorable little puppy (who is the love of her life, but shhhh...don't tell her husband).

Moneeka's clients find themselves inspired to take action and achieve massive success through her results-driven programs that also include having fun as part of the process. One of her clients recently said, "Run, don't walk, to take Moneeka's program. You will get so much more than you ever anticipated." She is the best-selling author of the book "Choose

Bliss: The Power and Practice of Joy and Contentment," which was recently honored with the very prestigious Woman of Impact Quill Award by Focus on Women Magazine.

She is also the host of the Podcast Real Estate Investing for Women where she focuses on all the aspects of real estate investing including strategies, mindset, emotional mastery, money smarts, and so much more, to ensure her listeners' success.

Moneeka's expertise, and blissful laugh, have been featured all over the world on stages, radio, podcasts, and TV stations including ABC, CBS, FOX, and the CW.

Moneeka@CoreBlissLife.com

www.Blissfulinvestor.com

www.CoreBlissLife.com

https://www.facebook.com/groups/Blissfulinvestor

https://www.facebook.com/MoneekaSawyer

https://twitter.com/MoneekaSawyer

https://www.linkedin.com/in/moneeka-sawyer-4561145/

The Final Gift
Dr. Ruth Anderson

My story is a journey that began with friendship. It was one of those friendships that was closer than family, fed me when my soul was hungry and meant more to me than life itself. *My best friend taught me that it was not only okay, but necessary, to step outside of my comfort zone and recreate how I view myself and how the world views me. I just wish she hadn't had to die for me to learn this lesson.*

Sylvia and I taught together in California and became fast friends in spite of the fact that I was 29 and Sylvia was 52. Even with our age difference, we both played the role of protective mother at times. When I divorced my husband, Sylvia was my emotional support, confidant, and companion. Soon thereafter, I moved to Colorado. I missed Sylvia terribly. Over the next 23 years, we spoke on the phone often and got together several times a year. I became the daughter Sylvia never had, and she was closer to me than the family I was born into.

One of our favorite traditions was preparing Thanksgiving dinner for 25 of our closest friends and family. Together we did the shopping, set tables, ordered flowers and prepared the food. November 2012, Sylvia called and told me she could not join me for Thanksgiving. Her brother was dying of cancer and she needed to stay close to him. Of course, I was crushed, but I completely understood.

That Thanksgiving morning, I awoke from a horrible, but very vivid dream where Sylvia's sister-in-law called me to tell me that Sylvia was in the hospital and fatally ill. I could not shake that sickening feeling all day. I tried to call Sylvia several times, but I could not reach her. The next morning, my dream became my real-life nightmare. Sylvia's sister-in-law called and said that Sylvia had had a massive stroke at the Thanksgiving table. She was in the hospital in Los Angeles. I flew to California to be with her and found that she was completely incapacitated. My beautiful

75-year-old friend was paralyzed on the left side of her body and was completely reliant on others.

Over the next few months, I received intuitive premonitions about Sylvia's health before she was diagnosed. I traveled from Colorado to be with her every few weeks and did my best to advocate for her health, comfort, and safety. Four months after her stroke, Sylvia passed away from stomach cancer. I was at her side as her soul transitioned to be with her loved ones. I thought my world ended then and there.

After she passed away, I was very aware of Sylvia's spirit. She visited me many times. Even my dog Jack was aware of her presence; he would respond by whining and sitting like a statue on the step she used to sit on to pet him. Not only could I feel her presence, but I could ask her questions and receive her answers. By communicating with her spirit-to-spirit, she helped me plan her Celebration of Life. I was beginning to understand that our souls don't die when our bodies do, and that ultimately, love transcends death.

As I picked up the shattered pieces of my existence, I held onto the last gift that Sylvia gave me: the need to understand the intuitive abilities that I witnessed during her illness and after her death. These experiences left me wondering. Why am I seeing and feeling these things while no one around me sees them? Does this mean I am psychic? The negative cultural perception connected to the word "psychic" had me spinning. What do I do with this? What do I want to do with this? If I want to explore it, what do I do and who do I do it with?

Hold on, I am a Christian. Growing up Methodist, I had heard skepticism about psychic or intuitive abilities. Doesn't the Bible state that this level of knowledge is wrong, or worse, evil? For something to be wrong doesn't there need to be an intention of wrongdoing? I never intended to be able to access psychic phenomena; it was just there. Did having this ability, whether it was wanted or not, distance me from God? The God I love and have a personal relationship with? I think the Bible would make us think so. I still went to church. And sometimes at church, I saw spirit forms that I did not intend or desire to see. How ironic. If seeing energy was wrong, why was it happening at church?

I had more questions than answers. I knew that if I wanted to understand my ability to connect with a spirit that no longer had a body, I needed to learn from others who had similar skills. I garnered the strength to seek out psychics that could explain what I had experienced. I met with four different energetic healers and they each suggested that I take classes in order to understand my intuition. I struggled with the idea of learning about clairvoyance. Meanwhile, my intuitive awareness continued to develop. Finally, I searched for a teacher I could trust and respect. Over the next three years, I devoted my time and energy to take intuitive classes and wallow in all things related to spiritual energy. I began to understand about Sylvia's presence in spirit form and I also saw that during my childhood I had had several intuitive experiences. Perhaps I was re-learning skills that I had already known. I learned about past lives and soul contracts. I took so many classes that I became a Reiki Master and a licensed minister.

I spent a lot of time in meditation. During meditation, I was presented with a ministry that I called **"Divine Healing at Open Clinic."** I was shown a place in the ethereal realm that was completely open; it had no walls and I knew there was going to be immense healing taking place there. I was told the name "Open Clinic," which made sense because souls could come and go. In my mind, it was open 24 hours a day, seven days a week. I later realized that in the spiritual realm there was no such thing as 'time,' as we know it. I was shown my higher self in a Minister's robe channeling God's divine healing light and holding space for the healing that would be taking place in this huge arena.

In meditation, I met and worked with Archangels Michael, Gabriel, Raphael and the Divine Mother. At Open Clinic, souls came and I saw the archangels and Divine Mother provide them grace, love, and healing. I learned how to intuitively read the stories that were taking place there. If I saw a gray energy mass, I knew that the soul had once been in a body and had passed away; the soul was still alive but no longer attached to a body. If I saw a white energetic mass, I knew that this was a soul that was there for healing and was still attached to a body in our physical realm. I was able to understand why each soul was there and what sort of healing they received whether it was on a spiritual, emotional, or physical basis. Once the souls received healing, they would return to their bodies on earth or back to the Cathedral of Souls where they would wait until the next lifetime.

Still, I struggled with the dichotomy of intuition and Christianity... a lot.
I shared my concerns with the archangels and with God. Several different times I was given the amazing gift of being in the divine presence of Jesus Christ. I was shown that my work with the archangels was indeed divinely blessed. I discovered and owned that the opinions that other people might have about my soul's future had no bearing on me or my work. My learning's continued. I was fascinated that *at death, our souls continued to live, continued to heal, and continued to learn.* I was being strongly guided to put this information into writing. Spirit encouraged me to create

a blog, then a website. Okay, created www.theministryonline.com. Then Spirit encouraged me to publish a book. I asked "What do you mean I am to go public about being intuitive, working with archangels, life after life, and receiving communication from loved ones who have passed over?" People will think I am mentally unstable. I had free will to say no, but I believed that these learnings needed to be shared. Okay, I did it. I wrote a book. *One Love: Divine Healing at Open Clinic* was put into the world. Lastly, I was led to speak about my experiences.

But wait a minute, I am an introvert!

Growing up, we were influenced by German and conservative Baptist lineage. We were encouraged to keep our thoughts to ourselves; to not take up a lot of space in the world, and not share our feelings with others. Religion and politics were private and not to be discussed, even within our home. My almost 30-year career as a teacher and school district administrator fit perfectly with my "don't show emotions" persona. I could keep my professional facade and keep others at arm's length. As a true introvert, this career choice worked very well for me.

I realized I didn't get to be an introvert if I was carrying a message from the archangels. I used to hold my religious beliefs very private. Well, not anymore. I not only needed to allow other people to see what I believed, but I was to purposefully invite them in to get a closer look! I knew that my beliefs challenged those of others, so I needed to prepare my psyche for condemnation while I was at it.

How was it that an introvert who consciously chose to have no voice was now stepping out and sharing a controversial platform on a global basis? It wasn't easy, but I did it! I lived it! I became the poster child for transformation, stepping into my own energy, living in authenticity, and embracing my brilliance. If anyone else thought it was brilliant or not, didn't matter. I was not trying to change anyone's mind about anything, just reporting what I had experienced. Like a drop of oil on water, sharing my energy and truth created an impact on the world. As I continued to put myself out there for others, my impact expanded.

I experienced a personal transformation that surprised me and those who knew me. My life during the past five years completely turned upside down. I would not have achieved that without Sylvia's final gift to me: spirit-to-spirit connection. *Sylvia's death resulted in a second death... a death of my old self in order for a new self to be able to emerge and develop.*

Is a person ever too old to start over? Is it ever too late to recreate the persona that one wants to share with the world? I started my second career, that of a writer, intuitive, and spiritual counselor in my mid-50's. God willing, I have another 25 good years that I can use to make an impact on the world. It is never too late to embrace one's calling and become all that one's soul was meant to be. The world needs each and every one of us to step into our brilliance. Someone needs to hear the message that you have to share.

What if your calling doesn't look anything like what you are doing now? Are you willing to question all that you believe, and let go of what you thought your life would be, to embrace limitless new possibilities? Every moment, every conversation, every decision, you have the opportunity to create yourself anew. Trust me, I know.

My Tips to Help You SHINE!

1. It's never too late to embrace one's calling.
2. The world needs each of us to step into our brilliance.
3. Someone needs to hear the message(s) that you have to share.
4. Be willing to embrace limitless new possibilities and SHINE!
5. Remember, every moment, every conversation, every decision, you have the opportunity to create yourself anew.

About the Author

Dr. Ruth Anderson is a lifelong student, teacher, and multi-award-winning author. Retired after a satisfying and worthwhile career in special education and public-school administration, Ruth was given the life-changing opportunity to redefine how she saw herself and grow into her soul's purpose. After a myriad of classes and hours meditating, she embraced her second calling, that of an author, intuitive, and transformational facilitator. Ruth walks in connection with Spirit and spends time daily listening to her angelic guides including Divine Mother, and Archangels Michael, Gabrielle, and Raphael. She freely shares the lessons that she has learned during her meditative sessions via her writing and with her clients.

Ruth is an ordained minister with The Church of Inner Light and uses her books, website, and Facebook to share her ministry of inspiring others to connect with their higher selves and embrace their soul's calling. Her goal is to live an authentic life that is worthy of her soul's calling and help transform lives through her work. Ruth lives in Colorado, adores her family and friends, and is passionate about her pets Tucker, Jack, Maddie, and Lola. Above all else, Ruth strives to make the world a more compassionate place.

Email: openclinic1@outlook.com

Phone number: (303) 726-7095

Website: www.theministryonline.com

Facebook: The Ministry Online

Twitter handle: TheMinistryRA

Lessons I learned from Fifth Street
Cassandra F. Garabedian

Growing up in Berkeley, California in the 1960's on the flatlands sometimes *referred* to as the "Waterfront", is where life came alive for me and many of my childhood friends. Fifth Street was a playground of sorts for us, with its cool breeze coming off the San Francisco Bay, hovering ever so gently in the air, it kept us from overheating as we gasped for air from running and playing as if our lives were dependent upon our every move. Occasionally you would hear the loud bang of several aluminum screen doors being hit simultaneously as if the houses were being attacked and under siege by a SWAT team, only to find it was a pack of eight to ten kids raiding two to three houses for snacks and Kool-Aid.

Right in the middle of Fifth Street, between Channing Way and Dwight Way in front of our houses is where we played, (traffic rarely came through on Fifth Street), it was our semi-private section of the "Waterfront". We were very imaginative and creative when it came to how we used our surroundings to fulfill our needs. We used the manhole in the street for our home base when we played softball or a game of kickball. If we wanted to play handball, we would play in the delivery driveway of one of the companies on Fifth Street, up against their huge roll-up door that faced the front of the building; perfect for a game of handball.

I will often reflect on my childhood and say, "we had the best of both worlds", we had Aquatic Park, one block behind us, and just across the railroad tracks, a trail we often would journey in search for wild black berries. The adventures we took together exploring the familiar surroundings with different expectations each time, or none at all; it was an enlightening time. **We were pure, honest, non-judgmental, and the best of friends, untainted kids enjoying the fruits of life and what life had to offer. It was life at its best.**

Sitting on prime real estate, we had a clear view of the iconic Golden- Gate Bridge and the Bay Bridge, as we raced on Schwinn Sting Ray bikes up and down the block. The bridge being iconic really didn't matter, what was important to us was our union and the pleasure we found in each other's company.

We played outside all day however, when the street lights came on everyone knew that was our cue to call it quits, say our good byes and go inside; it was bad news for you if your mama had to call you inside, and then everybody knew about it.

We played every game known to a child of this era, it fulfilled our wildest of dreams. **No dream was too big, the possibilities were endless, because we believed in our dreams, in fairy tales, in our parents and in God.**

Those were the golden years, when the entire neighborhood, "the village" part-took in the raising of the children in the neighborhood. There were times when we were a bit mischievous, like when we squeezed through the gate of a plant that manufactured aircraft parts stealing metal bits that resembled coins so that we could play store. Undoubtedly, when a neighbor saw us and told our parents we had to return what we had taken to the plant and explain how we got on to their property.

Everybody knew each other by name and the kids respected their elders and called them by their surnames, starting with Mr. or Mrs.

It was always fun during the holidays. Families would share their traditional meals/ ethnic meals: Mexican cuisine, French cuisine, Chinese cuisine, Japanese cuisine, traditional American and African American soul food. It was a feast to be enjoyed like no other!

Even the companies and corporations who had businesses located on or nearby Fifth Street gave back to the community by supporting our education and development in the sciences, social and economic development, contributing to building our character, establishing relationships outside of our comfort zone, and promoting good will. They held holiday parties and special science events solar nights that were similar to The Lawrence Hall of Science Observatory, and all of us kids were able to see and learn about the solar system, up close and personal, first hand and on Fifth Street.

These acts of kindness, of which there were many, left an everlasting positive impression of my childhood experience of how people of different backgrounds, ethnicities, religions and beliefs could raise their families in harmony. They lead by example, by showing respect for one another and treating one another with dignity. In many ways we were our own community, we looked out for one another. That being said, it was not unusual for our homes to be kept unlocked, so that we could run in and out of the house freely without disturbing our moms.

The gratitude I have for all the people who shared in my development, in me becoming the woman that I am, I bring forth part of you, because you live inside of me. I thank you for your priceless gifts, Fifth Street was good to me.

The moral of this story is, we were a diverse carefree group, living life to the fullest, enjoying each other's company to the max, totally oblivious to what was taking place outside of our safe haven.

We were nestled away from all the protesting and marching that was taking place in downtown Berkeley and on the U.C. Berkeley Campus; for the most part, we stood apart from the issues that in other places in America children, women and men of a different race were enduring social and economic injustice.

Race relations, social and economic inequality in the South all seemed so far removed from our everyday existence, yet it was hard to comprehend and ignore the violence we saw, the evening news reports, the vivid pictures of dogs being unleashed on people, people being beaten with clubs, people being hit with the force of water coming from hoses commonly used to fight fires and you ask the question why?

Martin Luther King Jr. helped many to come up with their answer to that burning question. In Berkeley we had many protests, there was one that comes to mind. It was the one where my sister and I, by accident got caught in a protest that turned into a riot. The Black Panthers were marching on Telegraph Avenue, near the U.C. Berkeley campus, my mom had finally allowed us to venture downtown to the record store and we come into a riot situation and got tear gassed. Eyes burning, coughing and trying to hold my sister's hand we managed to stay together as we ran in the opposite direction of all the chaos. For those few moments for the first time I felt, smelled, tasted, heard, and experienced the fear they knew all so well.

The years seem to roll by, friends from the neighborhood were graduating from Berkeley High School and moving away from their home of thirty-five years. One by one, like little birds our wings were being clipped for the test of life. Our childhood had afforded us "heaven on earth" for those precious years, a solid foundation in which to co-exist in harmony with nature and others. Now, we had to spread our wings, and in doing so spread the "Good News", by stepping up and living to the best of our abilities, according to the examples set forth by our parents. The choice was ours alone. We now have the freedom (free will) to choose if we will continue to respect and honor one another, to show human kindness and dignity towards one another no matter who or where he or she came from or their social-economic status. We must always remember where we came from.

Life has brought about a change, I am far from Fifth Street, far from Albany High School from where I graduated. Far from U.C. Berkeley, where I decided to take a leave of absence after my sophomore year in college to pursue an international modeling career.

I became the foreigner, walking the cobblestone streets in Milan, Italy! Milan became my home for the next two years while I lived out one of my dreams in real life. I got to walk the catwalk of the fashion houses of Milan. I had a fantastic run as a runway model, I had the pleasure to work with several "household name" designers. Not only did I get to work closely with the designers, but I got to be in close quarters, elbow to elbow with "top models" and I was considered a part of that group however, my upbringing wouldn't allow me to take on that "attitude". I was grateful for the wisdom that would seem to come at the right moments and which kept me grounded. Instead I learned all that I could from everyone who was willing to share their "bag of tricks" (tricks of the trade) which they had picked up through the years of modeling. We enjoyed sharing our treasures.

I remember a train trip to Venice and Rome where I found myself enjoying the food, the art, the architecture, the history, the people, and the fashion. I met so many people and gained new friendships. The differences in our languages wasn't a problem, because we didn't make it a problem. Through the language of love, happiness, joy, laughter, signs and body language, and bits of broken English mixed with Italian we were able to communicate just fine. It made for some fun afternoons and evenings. Soon we were teaching each other our language. I had the opportunity to learn how to cook several authentic Italian meals.

Before my years as a runway model, fashion had always been my passion and in my family. I felt honored to be able to work side by side my mother, Georgia Franklin a former head seamstress at Levi Strauss & Co., San Francisco. An entrepreneur in her own right, she was my mentor and inspiration. My mom taught me many things but, we had a greater connection then my siblings based on our love for fashion. We would spend hours together shopping for fabric and looking through Vogue, McCalls, and Butterick patterns. My mom could sew an outfit together with or without a pattern that could revival any "off the rack" garment from Bloomingdales or Saks Fifth Ave.

My childhood has prepared me for many of life's events, both good and bad. Knowing when to sow and when to reap has been my saving grace. It is comforting to know that during life's challenges there are lessons to be learned. Just like those days on Fifth Street when one of us were absent from school for 2 or more days, we depended on each other to pick up all missed homework and class assignments. That is how we looked out for each other. Today, I bring that same philosophy to my business.

I am a Style Consultant, CEO and the owner of Making Statements 'N Style. I am uniquely skilled in women's apparel and accessories. With over fifteen years' experience assisting women on Dressing for Success (note: fashion with a purpose). When I have the honor of working with an individual, together we create a poised, polished, put-together, effortless signature look that resonates confidence. The look would be instrumental in making the right impression at the right time, when it matters the most. I help their inner beauty, poise, and confidence be seen on the outside too so that they can make an authentic statement without saying a word.

<u>Highlights from My Spiritual Journey to Living and Shining your light out into the world:</u>

1. <u>Live in harmony</u>
2. <u>Enjoy and celebrate differences</u>
3. <u>Choose kindness and dignity</u>
4. <u>Run from chaos</u>
5. <u>Follow your dreams</u>
6. <u>Choose what matters</u>
7. <u>Remember you were chosen from on High</u>
8. <u>You were born to with intention and purpose</u>
9. <u>Only you can say, "I am"</u>
10. <u>Open your mind, your heart and soul allow the universal life-force to flow through you to heal, energize and recharge your physical body. Then give thanks.</u>

About the Author

Cassandra Garabedian is a style consultant, CEO and the owner of Making Statements 'N Style.

She has been in business for over fifteen years assisting women on how to dress for success while achieving their goals in life.

Cassandra, a former international runaway model brings a wealth of knowledge, skills, talents, tricks of the trade and gifts to women who are looking to take their image to the next level and want to become a better version of themselves. Cassandra will show her clients how to make magic out of their personal preferences and lifestyles. Clients also have the option of having all the details taken care of through her Personal Shopper's Program

Making Statements 'N Style is about an individual's inner beauty, their poised, put together, effortless and confident look that creates authentic fashion forward magic where no words are needed to describe the experience......IT SPEAKS FOR ITSELF!

For Twenty-two years Cassandra lead a successful career in Corporate America Financial Marketing Programs. She holds a BS degree in Business Management and in Marketing

She is currently a member with the Commonwealth Club, National Association of Women Business Owners, National Association of Professional Women, Women Speakers Association, and the Step Forward and Shine Community just to name a few.

Outside of her professional life she participates in a variety of organizations, such as the public

television network KQED, donating her time and cash to support their humanitarian drives, Love

A Child, the Center for Battered Women, Bay Point and her church, Unity Church of Richmond

with their food drives to help feed their cities homeless.

Cgarabedian53@gmail.com

510 755-5903

510 841-6800

www.makingstatementsnstyle.com

https://www.facebook.cypom/Making-Statements-N-Style-2053964941541986/

Leveraging that Magic Moment
Step into Your Light
Jeanne Alford

Picture this: You're at a cocktail party with friends, colleagues, your boss and a large group of local dignitaries. The group is discussing the latest current events and sharing laughs. You stand quietly, sipping your drink and hope that no one looks your way. What do you have to add to this conversation?

Fast forward a few hours. The party is over; you've completed the one-hour drive home. As you are unlocking your front door, a splendiferously funny retort pops into your head. "Why didn't I think of that?" you exclaim out loud. Welcome to the club!

The very idea of speaking up conjures up such fear. First your throat goes dry and tightens up. Your eyes bug out with fear and you pray no one notices. (At least that has been my experience!) Guess what? For the most part, no one sees your discomfort. They are too busy getting caught up in their own fears.

Something deep within you reminds you, "All you need to do is take a deep breath." Do you believe it? If not, you will soon. Because there is *magic* in that breathe, in that moment.

One of the things that people fear the most is public speaking. It's far more prevalent to say *speaking up* in public. You don't have to jump up on a stage to trigger this fear. You just need to be in a group of folks that you really want to like you! That said, with a little forethought, a little guidance and a lot of practice using that *magic moment*; we all can increase our confidence and speak up.

The very act of picking up a book like **Step Forward and Shine** shows an intention to conquer that fear. How do we address our fear of public speaking or speaking up in public—of *shining out loud*? We address it by remembering who we really are. In one of her most famous statements, Marianne Williamson states: "Our deepest fear is that we are powerful beyond measure." **Think about that. It's not that we fear we are inadequate; it's that we fear we are too much!**

With that in mind, I want to discuss a few steps that I have learned and taught that will help each of us step into our own spotlight. *Please note that I include myself as a recipient for this message.* We will look at the difference between just talking and communicating. Explore how planning and practice can help us overcome our fears, and share a few tips to make the journey easier.

Do you Talk?

I recently was conducting a workshop with Silicon Valley entrepreneurs and I started with a startlingly simple question: "Do you talk?"

I heard some giggles, caught a few quizzical looks and saw everyone's hands begin to reach for the sky. "Of course, we all talk," I said as I lifted my hand as well. "But do you communicate?" I watched as they once again had questioning looks and saw a few hands begin to go down. "Let me be more specific, do you know the difference?" I noticed, not surprised at all, that a remarkable number of hands dropped down.

While these two words are used interchangeably, we often don't consider their difference. *Talk* has a number of definitions, including "to communicate." It's a verb. It's a noun. It can be used with or without objects. It's an integral part of many idioms in the English language. *Talk* is a big word. *Communicate*, on the other hand, is a much more specific word. It's simply means "to impart knowledge, to exchange information."

I took it one more step with my audience. I explained, without exchanging information – making sure that the person or group we are interacting with received that information, it's just talk. I likened it to when I have a discussion with my computer. It's one way only. The dictation software hears me, types what I say, but cannot process it any further.

To communicate means someone got my information-they heard it, processed it, analyzed it and responded with their understanding.

Is it a reflex or an action?

To ensure that we communicate, we need to know what we want to impart. In other words, the first question to ask ourselves in that *magic moment* is,

"What do I want to say?" Why is that question important? If you don't know what you want to say, you will respond with what comes first to mind. Does that fit your agenda or move the discussion? Sometimes yes, but more often no. Think of the young child scolded for leaving a mess, "Who did this?" he's asked. "I dunno!" he cries out. It's an age-old scene in every household. The child doesn't want to be in trouble but doesn't have the skills yet to distract or divert, so he says the first thing. I heard that answer so many times raising my son...I once told him, "You get 'I dunno' in here to help you clean it up!" I call this a *shoot from the hip* response. It's more reflex than anything.

We each are inundated with messages every day. A study conducted by the University of California San Diego estimates that people are besieged with the equivalent of 34 gigabytes of information daily. That's a huge data dump that includes 105,000 words plus pictures, videos, games and so one. Another study showcased in *Adweek* shows an average social media user exposed to 285 pieces of content daily. Now that doesn't sound like a lot until you see that it includes a whopping 54,000 words and as many as 1,000 clicks and more than 7 hours of video. No wonder we are overwhelmed!

But are we getting the information that we need? Are we exchanging the thoughts and data necessary to move a discussion or project forward, or are we so overwhelmed that we only have time to react—to *shoot from the hip*—instead of to respond? Do you take a moment to contemplate how to respond to all this activity or do you fire off a response automatically? It's at this juncture—that nanosecond between hearing and seeing information and formulating your response—that I recommend we stop and take in that *magic moment*. In the time it takes for a good, deep breath, I tell my clients, "You let your brain catch up to your mouth. You allow yourself to ask, '*What do I want to say?*" **That moment, that breath, can change your response from a reaction to a deliberate, thoughtful reply.**

See from Other's Eyes: The Point of Perspective

As a communications expert, I can tell you, we have many platforms at our fingertips. With tools like Facebook and Twitter, it's not unusual to just shoot out our thoughts widely with no thought to how the recipient will process it. This is often referred to by my colleague, Kimi Avery, as "stuck in your own head syndrome." We assume our friends will hear what we have to say—see it from our point of view. We may not even consider what's going on with them or what their perception might be.

Taking time to consider other's perceptions is another step in strengthening our own communications skills and building confidence.

We all see the world from a unique point of view. This includes our own experiences, unique thoughts, lessons learned, beliefs and so on. Each of these aspects color how we interpret the information we encounter every day. With that in mind, think about how different your friends, family and colleagues see the world…different from the uniqueness of you.

Consider the old parable from India about six blind men and an elephant. Each man gets a chance to feel the elephant. One man, touching the leg, equates the elephant to a pillar. One, holding the tail, disagrees and says the elephant is a rope. The one closest to the trunk calls it a tree while the one by the ears thinks it's a big hand fan. The one near the belly declares an elephant is a huge wall and the one holding the tusk says it's a pipe. Six men, six different realities, one elephant.

An Effective Approach: Planning and Action

As we strive to step forward and shine, it's a great time to look at how we present ourselves to our clients, friends, colleagues and the public at large. When we take the audience into consideration it can enhance our communication. When we have a stronger connection and communicate clearly while serving our audience, it increases our confidence and let's our light shine even brighter. Taking the time to configure your message—your information—to answer what is the most important to your audience is a critical step in improving your communications effectiveness. This is true whether you are presenting a big business plan or simply chatting over coffee with your best friend.

But how can this be done? Again, it's a *magic moment* situation. While you take that deep breath, consider **"Why do they care?" "What will serve them?"**

Making the Journey a Breeze

For many skills, we rely on muscle memory. Think about riding a bike. We often don't think about putting our foot on a pedal and pumping. We just do it. If we stop to consider what we are doing, we run the risk of falling. At the beginning, however, we had to learn and practice how to ride a bike. Until we learned how to balance, we had help in the form of training wheels and parents holding us up.

Think about breathing—something we rarely think about. We rely on muscle memory to ensure we get our oxygen. But when we take the time to meditate or simply breathe deeply, it becomes a much more efficient, healthy action. Try it.

Both riding a bike and breathing are skills we practice into existence. We practiced so much when we started out that we don't even need to think about them today. Let me underscore that thought: *A process that we practiced into existence—into our muscle memory—to become part of our everyday activities.*

Deliberate and thoughtful communication can also become muscle memory. It takes practice and planning. Planning, so you know what to communicate and what action you want to come from your communication. Practice, so you can build it into that muscle memory. A deliberate, thoughtful focus aids each of us as we strive to get out in front of that daily data onslaught. Taking that *magic moment* deep breath allows each of us to consider the "who, what and why's" of our communications in a nanosecond. It sounds like a lot of effort, but, like riding a bike and breathing, with practice it becomes second nature.

My advice to clients, once we pull together a speech or presentation is this: **Practice.** I've told them to practice in the mirror as they prepare for the morning. Practice while commuting home. Practice inside your head and practice out loud. Then I say, "Once you think you have it down, practice one more time!" The more you practice, the easier it is—like riding a bike and breathing deeply. With each modicum of improvement comes more confidence. With practice, you will feel much more comfortable in speaking up at the next cocktail party.

Letting others see your brilliance is imperative. You have a light that the world needs today. Only you can uncover it and share it. **I encourage you to enjoy the process and SHINE.**

About the Author

An experienced speaker, trainer, writer and PR expert, Jeanne Alford spent her career honing her expertise in communications. She has directed national and international public affairs and public relations programs for several brands including Dolby, Philips Electronics and Visa. She has also worked with leaders at some of the most innovative start-ups in Silicon Valley. No matter what position she held, her focus remains on telling a compelling branding story.

Jeanne's communications and PR campaigns have changed media perceptions, garnered national and international awareness for issues and helped to strongly position executives as industry leaders. As an advocate for employee communications and crisis communications, she led programs to ensure that a company's most important asset, its people, is kept informed. As a trainer, she has assisted many executives in refining and leveraging their media efforts to ensure their company story is told through the eyes of respected media writers and broadcasters.

Today, Jeanne works with individuals and small businesses to tell their most captivating stories – in the media, with customers and among their colleagues. As a communications and media coach, she strives to apply those skills so her clients can tell their best stories using the most effective platforms. Her focus is on developing communications strategies and coaching business leaders to elevate and refine their message.

Jeanne, a best-selling co-author and writer, published several business articles, white papers and marketing campaigns. Her materials have appeared in daily newspapers, national business publications and on several online sites. She most recently authored "3 Magic Questions to Instantly Improve Your Communications," which is available to download at BeClear101.com

Email: jeanne@beclear101.com

Phone: 415-971-3344

Websites: alfordcommunications.com, beclear101.com

Facebook: https://www.facebook.com/BeClear101-1896566077223594/

LinkedIn: https://www.linkedin.com/in/jeannealford

Twitter: @jealford

From Garbage to Gold
Kari Kelley

"My eyesight is flawed but my vision is perfect"
~ Kari Kelley

I sat in the back of the room holding my white cane folded in my lap. My sunglasses were on my face and my head was covered in a black scarf. I wore two garbage bags that I had fashioned to cover up my clothes. I listened as the emcee made announcements and urged everyone to make sure their cell phones were turned off. I listened to the bio that I had written and re-written numerous times before I took a deep breath and pressed send on the email. **My heart was beating loudly in my ears. I felt excited as well as a nervous wreck when I heard "Please welcome to the stage, Kari Kelley."**

I stood up, unfolded my cane and made my way to the front of the room. While the audience clapped, the plastic of my garbage bag costume rustled as I walked. The clapping stopped once I stepped on stage. I felt all eyes on me. I started singing 'Amazing Grace' and I changed the lyrics to "I am blind but I can see." I fold up my cane and take my sunglasses off and put them aside. I share with the audience how I lost some of my eyesight. "When I was fourteen months old I was shaken and while I was being shaken my head was bumped. I didn't get medical attention for ten days after this incident. Over that ten days fluid was building up on my brain. I was hospitalized and one shunt was placed in my head (I place my fingers on the place on my neck where the shunt can slightly be seen) and one shunt in my abdomen." (There is a scar on my abdomen but I don't show that one.)

I am clear that not every child survives shaken baby syndrome, but I did. There are countless children that suffer head injuries like mine but don't live to recover. So, this is where I say "My body was shaken but my spirit was not stirred. Even at fourteen months old being hard headed probably saved my life." (This line gets a few laughs.)

Next, I talk about my earliest memory of being a four-year-old child living in a foster home. My foster mother was putting icing on a cake and explaining to me that since today is my birthday I am four. I vividly remember putting my hands on my hips and stomping my foot and proclaiming "I'm three". Four months after that I am adopted into a new family.

This new family teaches me things about myself that I never knew before. A few things they taught me was; about my appearance. I have an overbite which they call "buck teeth." My skin color is referred to as "piss colored." With my damaged eyesight I endure countless insults from the usual "four eyes" although I didn't wear glasses much, to "cross eyed" and having people hold up fingers in front of me and asking "How many fingers am I holding up blind-y."

My hair is hard to manage so I hear how 'nappy headed' I am. However, when my mother is combing my hair I must cry silently and try not to flinch. I learned the first day my new parents picked me up from my foster home that my feelings of discomfort were not to be expressed out loud in my mother's presence. Her cruel command from the front seat of the car to her four-year-old daughter crying in the back to "shut up all that noise" was my early warning system. So, I dreaded having my mother pick up a comb and brush. Getting my hair done on Sunday morning was especially painful. My stomach would start churning when I heard my mother open the kitchen drawer where the pressing comb, what I refer to as 'torture instruments' was kept. I would sit in my room and listen to the scraping of the chair as she positioned it next to the stove and lit the flame on the stove.

She would call my name and I would make the long walk down the hall to the chair by the stove and try to focus on the gospel music playing from the stereo in the living room. At the end of this ordeal I would have beautiful straightened shiny hair for church. Eventually I would spend almost an entire Saturday every six weeks in a beauty salon for the same beautiful straightened shiny hair until my mother found someone to put corn rows that were almost as painful as the pressing comb in my hair. When I was about ten years old my mother had a stroke that left her paralyzed on her right side. She was no longer able to do my hair herself nor was she always able to pay others to do it so I wore wigs occasionally.

The children had lots of fun snatching it off and playing 'keep away' with it.

I learned that I was a "stupid, ugly half blind child that was good for nothing." For years I believed this was true. I was not an especially good student. School was always challenging for me. Having poor eyesight and dealing with abuse at home was quite a struggle. My mother died the summer before I went to the eighth grade. All during high school I did more cutting classes or not showing up at school at all. Eventually I had to tell my father that I was not graduating with my class. He proceeded to order me into the car and drove me to a place in the neighborhood where drug addicts, prostitutes, alcoholics and other unsavory characters were in plain sight. **He told me that one or all of these conditions would be my future and that he always knew that I would "never amount to nothing." I believed him and found myself living a life that invited destruction on many levels.**

I engaged in a lot of reckless behavior. I attracted men that didn't treat me well, however, I never experienced domestic violence and I didn't fall into prostitution. I tried lots of different drugs; however, I never became addicted. I have a soft spot in my heart for vodka; however, I am not an alcoholic. I felt depressed and alone more often than not. Drugs, alcohol and relationships could never completely fill the hole inside. I sought out therapy and anti-depressants. I even threw myself into religion(s). All these proved to be temporary fixes.

Today I recognize the inner spark that stayed lit as my life's challenges took me through dark places. The spirit that didn't stir while my fragile body was shaken contained that spark. That spark stayed lit as I believed the people telling me that I was less than and my feelings were not to be expressed. Even as I walked with my head down and covered my mouth when I laughed or smiled that spark stayed lit. **That spark stayed lit** during every dysfunctional relationship. That spark stayed lit through all the drugs and alcohol that littered my body. The spark never went out as I spent hour after hour in office after office of psychologist and/or psychiatrist. That spark stayed lit as I filled prescription after prescription of anti-depressant medication. That spark didn't die when I turned my back on one religion after another because I didn't know the difference in having a relationship with my Creator versus following what amounted to checking things off of a to do list in order to make sure I was living 'right.'

That spark began to grow into a flame when I found a definition of forgiveness that gave me freedom. This definition made it possible for me to measure how much I was going to continue suffering over all of the abuse that happened to me. Now I choose how many days I stay in bed crying over the loss of my innocence and the lack of parental love and support. I choose to spend as little of my time and energy thinking about my past abusers and the abuse they inflicted on me. I choose to believe that none of them are losing any sleep over how they treated me. However, I do believe that people that abuse their power over the powerless will answer for what they have done.

I stand on stage telling the audience about the flame that has turned into a raging fire that fuels my passion to let anyone still suffering from childhood abuse that it is possible to heal. I think of all of the words that were said to me that made me believe that I was nothing but garbage **I dramatically rip one of the two garbage bags off of me, wad it up and throw it across the room and say "<u>those words were garbage not me.</u>"**

When I think of all the events that made me feel like garbage I dramatically rip the second garbage bag off, throw it across the room and say "I deserve better than being treated like garbage." I remove the black scarf from my head and toss it behind me. The scarf doesn't wad up and go flying like the garbage bags do. I say "I will no longer treat my life like garbage." Hidden beneath the garbage bags and scarf is a beautiful golden outfit that makes me look and feel like a priceless gem.

You too are a priceless gem, no matter what others have told you or you perhaps have told yourself. I encourage you to embrace the precious gift that you are and be willing to SHINE no matter what. Share the gift you of you…. don't let your spark blow out. Take the garbage bags off and SHINE!

I enjoy sharing my message of hope and healing for adult survivors of childhood abuse. **I am committed to encouraging any one that knows of a child in an abusive situation to do whatever it takes to get that child to safety.** I will not shy away from letting a predator know that he or she will have to answer for what they have done. *During my own journey I found that opening my heart to unconditionally loving my-self was the key to letting go of bitterness and anger that I was holding against those who hurt me.* Once all of the bitterness and anger was gone I got a clear vision of healing for everyone that had abused me. I felt my heart open and in my mind's eye I had a powerful vision of them standing in front of me, one by one I saw them stand up straighter and smile brightly after I looked them in their eyes, put my hands on their shoulders and said

"I knew that you were broken and you had no idea what you were doing. I love you and I forgive you."

My eyesight is not perfect but my vision is. Amazing grace is available. I close by telling the audience that "I have enough eyesight to get in trouble but not enough to get a driver's license." The audience laughs and I take a bow.

Now, I invite you to embrace the truth that you are a precious gem, worthy of love, protection, forgiveness and celebration. I encourage you to *open your heart to unconditionally loving yourself and let go of any bitterness and anger that you are holding against those who hurt you. Take off your garbage bags (the ways that we hide) and SHINE!*

About the Author

Kari Kelley is a writer, speaker and vocalist deeply passionate about sharing her voice of courage and inspiration. She has been featured on a wide variety of stages, panels, radio and TV shows across the United States. Kari is the author of "Black, Blind and Female" the creator, producer and performer of her one-woman shows "Somebody Else's Child," "Voices of Resilience" and "Three Chairs" and a contributing author to the bestselling e-book Village Pearls: Spiritual Practices to Uplift your Soul and the No. 1 Amazon bestselling book Heal Thy Self.

Kari has entertained VIPs at sold-out networking events all around Northern California.

karikelleyk2@yahoo.com

Twitter https://twitter.com/Karionk2

Linkedin https://www.linkedin.com/in/kakelley?trk=hp-identity-name

Facebook: https://www.facebook.com/voicesofresilience/

A Note From Rebecca

Dear Powerful Reader,

Thank you for reading our anthology. I hope it has touched your heart and spirit; encouraging and inspiring you to Step Forward and SHINE!

I wanted to share a little bit more about our organizations, Your Purpose Driven Practice™ and RHG Media Productions™. We are passionate about helping others live on purpose and with purpose in their life and business. I hope this book has supported and inspired you to choose to live on purpose, bloom and SHINE!

If you are wanting to reach more people and be part of inspiring and supporting others with your message, your gifts, and the work that you bring to the world; then I want to share some opportunities for you to consider.

Each year we compile and produce anthology book projects, support authors in publishing their own powerful books as best sellers, produce and publish an international magazine, launch TV shows, facilitate women's empowerment conferences, launch radio and podcast shows, help experts and speakers step into a place of powerful influence to make a global difference. We provide programs and strategies to help you reach more people, and facilitate the Speaker Talent Search (which helps speakers, experts, and influencers connect with more speaking opportunities.) We would love to support you in reaching more people. Please take a moment to learn a little bit more about us at the sites listed below, and then reach out to us for a conversation. **We would love to have you join us as we seek to make a positive global difference.**

You can learn more about each of these things are our main website: www.YourPurposeDrivenPractice.com

Enjoy our powerful **TV and podcast shows**:

www.RHGTVNetwork.com

Learn more about the **Speaker Talent Search™**:

www.SpeakerTalentSearch.com

Learn more about our **writing opportunities**:

http://yourpurposedrivenpractice.com/writing-opportunities/

If you would like to connect with me personally to explore some of our opportunities in upcoming book projects, podcast/radio shows, and/or TV, then here is the link to schedule a time to speak with me directly: www.MeetWithRebecca.com or you can email me at: Rebecca@YourPuposeDrivenPractice.com

May you always choose to Step Forward and SHINE!

Warmly,

Rebecca Hall Gruyter

Reviews

Linda F. Patten

When a group of powerful women such as the authors in this third book in the SHINE series come together, what they create is truly magic. Each one tells a story that is touching, poignant, funny and definitely uplifting. However, the true value is in the wisdom of each author's work and teachings. Each message provides key steps and strategies to bring profound change not only in our lives but in the world as well. To me as a leadership trainer, these authors inspired the leaders, influencers and movement makers within us all.

~ Linda F. Patten, Leadership Trainer for Women Entrepreneurs and Changemakers – President &CEO, Dare2Lead With Linda

Website: www.dare2leadwithlinda.com,
email: linda@dare2leadwithlinda.com

Additional Contact Information:

website: www.dare2leadwithlinda.com
https://www.facebook.com/dare2leadwithlinda
https://www.facebook.com/linda.patten.311
https://twitter.com/patten_linda
https://www.linkedin.com/in/lindapatten

http://www.youtube.com/c/LindaPatten

https://plus.google.com/+LindaPatten

https://www.pinterest.com/lindapatten311/

Cynthia Stott

If you have a message and gifts to share but are held back by fear and doubt, then Step Forward and SHINE is for YOU! It is truly an inspired and inspiring book. Chock full of amazing stories of transformation, it inspires you to move forward with powerful action steps in every chapter. If you have a mission or a calling that's been laid upon your heart, don't wait. Read this book and take your action steps. We need you. Your time is NOW.

~ Cynthia Stott

International Speaker Coach/Global Visibility Influencer

www.CynthiaStott.com

Programs@CynthiaStott.com

415.298.73

Olivia Parr-Rud

"Rebecca Hall Gruyter has done it again! Her new anthology, "Step Forward and SHINE", is a choir of inspiring voices that offer deep healing and powerful wisdom. If you feel called to share your unique gifts but find yourself blocked or unsure of your next step, then this book is for you. With heartwarming stories and ingenious strategies, Rebecca's contributors offer inspiration and tactics for every area of life. From physical wellness to emotional health to spiritual growth to financial freedom, this book is a great resource for your next step on your journey to realizing your highest potential – to truly "Step Forward and SHINE."

~ Olivia Parr-Rud, MS Corporate Love Ambassador

https://www.facebook.com/LoveMakeItYourBusiness/

610 563-8866 (Mobile)

215 948-3500 (Office - message only)

Dr. Cheryl Lentz

"The greatest desire we have is to be needed and called to make a difference in the lives of others. Make a difference in the world by saying yes to inner wisdom; make a difference in the world by saying yes to you in leading change. Make a difference by saying yes to adding this book to your library. Let this book inspire you to inspire others."

~ Dr. Cheryl Lentz

The Academic Entrepreneur
International Best Selling Author

VoiceAmerica Radio Talk Show Host
The Refractive Thinker® Press, where discriminating scholars publish.
www.RefractiveThinker.com
www.DrCherylLentz.com
Cell: 702 719 9214

Rita Milios

Deep inside, most of us want to shine, but lack of self-confidence and lack of encouragement often get in the way. The value of this book comes from the enlightening insights and bits of wisdom contained within the deeply personal stories shared by the book's contributors. I appreciate that these nuggets stand out, via the use of bolded text and/or lists. I'll be returning to these wisdom points again and again.

~ Rita Milios, LCSW, The Mind Mentor, Transformational Psychotherapist and Spiritual Coach; LinktoEXPERT: RitaMilios.linktoexpert.com

LinkedIn: https://www.linkedin.com/in/rita-milios-92b47576/

Rev. Laura Jackson Loo

Step Forward and Shine is an extraordinary anthology of personal triumph. There are powerful stories about how simple acts can change lives. In other cases, it's about the courage to face and overcome incredible odds to conquer physical or emotional circumstances. Whatever their personal story, this book is filled with countless empowering stories about learning how to honor yourself, your true gifts, and your true purpose of love, compassion and infinite potential.

~ Rev. Laura Jackson Loo

New Paradigm Thought Leader

Speaker, Author, Musician, Coach

www.laurajacksonloo.com

info@laurajacksonloo.com

804-818-6084

Located in Hampton Roads, Virginia

Closing Thoughts

I hope you have been touched by these powerful chapters and that they have encouraged, equipped and empowered you to step forward in powerful ways! We hope you have been encouraged on your journey and are inspired to apply the practical and profound tips, advice, and great wisdom into your life. We can't wait to see you, hear from you, and celebrate you as you share the gift of you with the world! May you always choose to Step Forward and SHINE!

****

Books compiled or written by Rebecca Hall Gruyter to be released in 2018 and 2019:

Empowering YOU, Transforming Lives

This anthology features over 36 authors helping you 365 days a year. This daily inspiration will give you great encouragement, love, support and insights to walk beside you every day of the year. Each day, we encourage you to stop, pause and reflect on the daily inspiration. Our goal and vision for this book is to have it encourage, inspire and empower you every single day of the year to support you in living your life on purpose and with great purpose. (To be released December 4, 2018.)

The Expert and Influencers Series: Leadership Edition

This powerful anthology will feature over 25 experts and influencers committed to empowering you in the area of Leadership. They will share tips, advice, powerful insights to help you step forward as a leader in your life and in your business. (To be released June 2019)

Step Into Your Brilliance!

This anthology featuring over 25 authors (the first book in the "Step Into" anthology series) will empower readers to discover and embrace their brilliance. This book will then equip and empower the reader to share their own brilliance with the world. The world needs you and your brilliance! (To be released in September of 2019).

The Animal Legacies!

This anthology featuring over 20 authors will share heart-warming, inspiring, empowering true stories of how animals have powerfully touched their lives. They will share a profound lesson they learned, a powerful truth, a powerful legacy, encouraging messages, a celebration and honor of our animal friends. Every reader will be encouraged, their heart touched; as each writer shares and passes to you their own animal legacy. We know this book will touch your heart and life. (To be released December 2019).

****

Anthologies Available Now Featuring Compiled by Rebecca Hall Gruyter:

Special **"SHINE Series"** (Compiled and led by Rebecca Hall Gruyter)

"Come out of Hiding and SHINE!" (Book 1 in the SHINE Series)

"Bloom Where You are Planted and SHINE!" (Book 2 in the SHINE Series)

"Step Forward and SHINE!" (This book, the 3rd and final book in the SHINE Series)

"The Grandmother Legacies" (Anthology Compiled by Rebecca Hall Gruyter)

****

Books Available Now Featuring a Chapter by Rebecca Hall Gruyter:

"The 40/40 Rules" Anthology compiled by Holly Porter (Nov 2018)

"Becoming Outrageously Successful" Anthology compiled by Dr. Anita Jackson

"Catch Your Star" Anthology published by THRIVE Publishing

"Discover Your Destiny" Anthology compiled by Denise Joy Thompson

"I Am Beautiful" Anthology compiled by Teresa Hawley-Howard

"The Power of Our Voices, Sharing Our Story" Anthology, compiled by Teresa Hawley-Howard

"Succeeding Against All Odds" Anthology compiled by Sandra Yancey

"Success Secrets for Today's Feminine Entrepreneurs" Anthology compiled by Dr. Anita Jackson

"Unstoppable Woman of Purpose" Anthology and workbook, compiled by Nella Chikwe

"Women on a Mission" Anthology compiled by Teresa Hawley-Howard

"Women of Courage, Women of Destiny" Anthology compiled by Dr. Anita Jackson

"Women Warriors Who Make It Rock" Anthology compiled by Nichole Peters

"You Are Whole, Perfect, and Complete - Just As You Are" compiled by Carol Plummer and Susan Driscoll

www.ingramcontent.com/pod-product-compliance
Lightning Source LLC
Chambersburg PA
CBHW022215090526
44584CB00012BB/568